Cook Well, Eat Well

Cook Well, Eat Well

RORY O'CONNELL

GILL BOOKS

Gill Books
Hume Avenue
Park West
Dublin 12
www.gillbooks.ie

Gill Books is an imprint of M.H. Gill and Co.

978 07171 7564 2

Designed by Graham Thew
Photographed by Joanne Murphy www.joanne-murphy.com
Styled by Orla Neligan of Cornershop Productions
www.cornershopproductions.com
Assistants to Orla and Rory: Bella Supiana, Pauline Sugrue,
Jessie Madigan
Edited by Kristin Jensen
Indexed by Eileen O'Neill
Printed by BZ Graf, Poland

PROPS
Avoca: www.avoca.ie
Meadows & Byrne: www.meadowsandbyrne.com
Marks & Spencer: www.marksandspencer.ie
Article Dublin: www.articledublin.com
Dunnes Stores: www.dunnesstores.com
Harold's Bazaar: 087 7228789
TK Maxx: www.tkmaxx.ie
Golden Biscotti Ceramics: http://goldenbiscotti.bigcartel.com
Industry Design: www.industrydesign.ie
Sostrene Grene: sostrenegrene.com
TWI Fabrics Ireland: fabricsireland.com
Flying Tiger Stores: ie.flyingtiger.com

This book is typeset in 12 on 13.5pt Portrait Regular.
The paper used in this book comes from the wood pulp of
managed forests. For every tree felled, at least one tree is
planted, thereby renewing natural resources.
A CIP catalogue record for this book is available from the
British Library.

5 4 3 2 1

Acknowledgements

When you are writing a book, sometimes it can feel like a rather solitary exercise, but in reality it takes a lot of helping hands to bring the printed article to fruition. Thank you to all who have been a part of the process. Nicki Howard, Teresa Daly, Catherine Gough and all at Gill Books – it has been a pleasure to work with you. Thank you Kristin Jensen for your editing and being gentle with me. Thank you Joanne Murphy and Orla Neligan for the wonderful photographs – it was a lot of fun. Thank you Graham Thew for the smart and clear design.

In my kitchen in Cork, Blo Deady helped me test recipes and brought many delicious ideas to the book. Noreen and Rachel Dunne and Bella Supiana provided all manner of invaluable help and support. Betty Lewis keeps my surroundings in order in a way I could never manage – thank you, Betty.

Thank you as ever to all of the team at the Ballymaloe Cookery School for your continued support.

Contents

Summer

Autumn

Winter

Larder

Introduction

I sometimes get asked, 'How do I create a balanced menu?'
Or people will say to me, 'I am never confident about
what I should serve with what.' This is what this book is
all about. As a result of those questions, I have composed
a series of seasonal balanced menus that I hope will be of
help to all cooks who find themselves in a similar position of
uncertainty.

The object of the exercise when creating a balanced meal is
to compose a menu that will nourish and delight and that
will leave diners feeling satisfied rather than overfed and
exhausted.

Almost all of the meals in this book are three courses, or
based on a starter, main course and generally something
sweet to end the meal. I suggest vegetable accompaniments
and sometimes salads to serve with main courses, but of
course individual elements of each meal can be eaten as a
less involved affair. Some of the recipes can be used over
multiple seasons by the simple change of an ingredient to
suit the season you are cooking in.

There are some guidelines to remember when planning a
meal, but for me the starting point is always the season I
am cooking in, as that determines to a great extent what
the content of the meal will be. When you cook the foods
of a particular season you get the best possible quality,
hopefully local ingredients and definitely the best value
for money. The sometimes forgotten irony of great food is
that when food is in season, it is at its best and also at its
least expensive. Cooking firmly with the seasons is also the
most sustainable approach and you will be supporting local
producers in your part of the world who are getting their
peak harvest to the market.

Not all ingredients can be local unless you are following a laudable but rigid and difficult policy of using only the food of your terroir. I would have great difficulty cooking without olive oil, lemons, spices, and exotic fruit at a time of the year when local fruit is not available, and so on, but I only use them to embellish what is best around me at that time.

At the end of the day, what most of us want is something nourishing and delicious to eat, and whether it is cooking for myself or a group of family or friends, cooking and then sharing the results of that effort remains a great pleasure.

Spring

If you can make an omelette, which is fast food in the best sense of the word and such a useful skill, then you can pretty much feed yourself.

Mussels are tremendously good value and grow in abundance around our coast. Though not normally associated with a filling for an omelette, I think they are great here. Wild garlic, another ingredient that grows abundantly, is one of my favourite spring ingredients and in this meal it also makes an appearance in the omelette. I love the idea of a free food that is so full of flavour and at the same time really good for you. Every season will have countless delicious treats to put in or to serve alongside the eggs. Later on in spring, the sprouting broccolis, sea kale and asparagus are real treats and I always look forward to mild spring lamb kidneys, which for me make one of the best omelette fillings of the year.

The meatballs take a bit of time to prepare, but it can all be done ahead of time and the final assembly is quick and easy. There is something rather wonderful about bringing a large dish of goodness to the table to be served family style, and meatballs have that slightly whimsical feel to them that just adds to the fun. A big bowl of spaghetti served alongside would heighten the feeling of jollity, but the grilled bread I suggest is also really good and perfect for mopping up the delicious juices. In many ways we have forgotten how important bread was as a daily staple, as the quality of bread that is generally available has deteriorated over the last 40 years. However, in the last few years a number of micro bakeries have popped up all over the country and determined young, and indeed older, bakers are hell bent on producing beautiful loaves that make you remember why bread was once referred to as the staff of life. Try to find the best bread you can for grilling and the quality of the olive oil is equally important. Ordinary bread and poor olive oil are not going to make the experience in any way special.

Meringue is a crowd pleaser in the best sense of the word, and in this case, with the addition of the tender poached green gooseberries and the butterscotch sauce, it adds up to a rather luscious confection. The seasonal elderflower perfumes the dish, and when the flower heads are available for decoration, it makes a fresh and beautiful presentation. The almond praline is a marvellous technique to master and can be ground to a fine powder or a coarse gravel-type consistency.

Mussel and Wild Garlic Omelette

16 fresh mussels

1 sprig of fresh thyme

50ml dry white wine

3 tablespoons cream

1–2 tablespoons finely chopped wild garlic leaves or fresh chives

4 free-range eggs

sea salt and freshly ground black pepper

10g butter

1 teaspoon extra virgin olive oil

1 dessertspoon wild garlic flowers or chive flowers, if available, to garnish

*This is a simple starter or lunch dish, though it is important to point out that the omelette must be eaten the moment it is cooked. The wild garlic can be replaced with finely chopped chives when the garlic is out of season. The fresher the eggs are for your omelette, the more delicious it will be. Be careful not to overcook the omelette or it will become hard and tough and lose its delicate, tender texture. I like some of the mussels to be visible when it arrives at the table, so I scatter a few over the cooked omelette. If I am having this as a lunch dish, I serve it with a simple leaf salad dressed with an olive oil vinaigrette (page 49). When served as a starter, as in this meal, I serve it with thinly sliced brown bread and butter. **Serves 2***

1   To check that all the mussels are fresh and alive before cooking, ensure they are tightly closed. If some of the shells are slightly open, tap them on your worktop – if they don't show signs of movement and appear to be closing, then leave them for a moment. Tap the ones you are unsure of again, and if there are still no signs of life, discard them. It is not crucial to remove the mussel's little hairy beard before cooking, as you will have the chance to do that when removing the meat from the shell when cooked.

2   Place the mussels, thyme and wine in a **small low-sided saucepan and cover with a tight-fitting lid**. I sometimes use a Pyrex plate as the lid so that I can see the mussels opening. Place on a gentle heat and cook for a few minutes, until the mussels have popped open. **It may be necessary to remove the opened mussels from the pan at intervals as invariably they never all open at the same time.** Be careful not to overcook the mussels or they will become shrivelled and tough.

3 If some of the mussels refuse to open, just discard
   them, as occasionally they are full of fine sand that
   will spoil your dish. As with any shellfish, use and
   trust your sense of smell. If any of the mussels smell
   strong and fishy and not sweetly fresh, then discard
   those too.

4 Sieve the mussel cooking liquid, return it to
   the saucepan, raise the heat and reduce by half.
   Add the cream and allow to bubble and reduce
   again to achieve a slightly syrupy or light coating
   consistency. Allow to cool.

5 Debeard the mussels by removing the little tuft of
   fibrous hair, then remove the mussels from the shells.
   Add them to the liquid along with the chopped wild
   garlic leaves and give them a gentle stir to mix. This
   can now be chilled for reheating later.

6 When you are ready to make the omelette, place
   a heavy non-stick or cast iron pan on a high heat.
   Have a warm but not scalding-hot serving plate
   ready. Beat the eggs thoroughly but don't overdo
   it – if the eggs become too airy, the texture of the
   cooked omelette will be bubble filled and won't be
   as good. Season with salt and pepper.

7 Reheat the mussels on a very **gentle** heat to just
   warm them through.

8 Add the butter and olive oil to the omelette pan.
   Swirl to cover the base of the pan and to coat the
   sides to a height of 3cm. Make sure the butter
   is **sizzling hot** before adding all the beaten egg
   mixture in one go. Swirl the liquid egg around the
   bottom of the pan to create an even layer. Holding
   the handle of the pan in one hand and an egg slice
   in the other, tilt the pan away from you. With the
   aid of the slice, distribute the liquid egg to ensure it
   cooks quickly and evenly. Draw the cooked omelette
   from the sides of the pan towards the centre as you

go and allow the uncooked and still liquid egg to run to the edges, where it will cook more quickly. Swirl any remaining uncooked egg around the edge of the pan to finish cooking it. The omelette should be cooked in about **15 seconds**.

9 Remove the pan from the heat and quickly add three-quarters of the mussels, placing them in a line along the middle of the omelette from one side to the other. Fold over the omelette and slide it onto the warmed plate. Spoon the remaining mussels and sauce over the omelette, garnish with wild garlic or chive flowers and **serve immediately**.

Chermoula Meatballs with Roasted Red Onions, Cherry Tomatoes and Green Olives

6 red onions, peeled and quartered

6 tablespoons extra virgin olive oil

2 sprigs of fresh thyme

sea salt and freshly ground black
  pepper

2 white onions, peeled and finely
  chopped

2 large garlic cloves, peeled and
  crushed to a paste

450g minced belly or shoulder of
  pork

450g minced chicken, preferably a
  mixture of both white and brown
  meat

70g fresh white breadcrumbs

1 egg, lightly beaten

3 tablespoons chermoula (page 15)

2 tablespoons grated Parmesan

2 tablespoons chopped fresh
  flat-leaf parsley

2 tablespoons chopped fresh
  marjoram

600g cherry tomatoes, peeled and
  seasoned with salt, pepper and
  caster sugar

550ml chicken stock (page 257)

To finish

50g green olives, stoned and
  coarsely chopped

zest of 1 lemon

3 tablespoons chopped fresh
  flat-leaf parsley

To serve

grilled sourdough bread (page 16)

Meatballs can be so satisfying and also convenient, as pretty much all the work can be done in advance. Chermoula, the paste used to flavour the meatballs, is a North African spice mixture that has hundreds of different uses and is a tremendously handy condiment to have in your fridge. I sometimes drizzle a little of it over a fried egg or rub a mackerel fillet with it before roasting or frying. Leftover cooked potatoes given a light crush then a drizzle of the paste and roasted until crispy are terrific. Cooked green beans, courgettes, broccoli and cauliflower also lap it up.

If you would like to prepare this dish ahead, you can assemble it, ready for the oven, but don't add the hot chicken stock until you are about to put it into the oven to cook.

Serve the meatballs with grilled sourdough bread and a salad of bitter leaves or with the spaghetti and courgettes on page 119. **Serves 8**

1 Preheat the oven to 200°C.
2 Toss the red onions in 2 tablespoons of the olive oil. Add the thyme and season with salt and pepper. Place in a single layer on a roasting tray and cook in the oven for about 30 minutes, until just tender. Reserve for the final assembly of the dish.
3 Heat another 2 tablespoons of olive oil in a heavy-bottomed saucepan, then add the chopped onions and garlic. Toss to coat in the oil and **cover** with a piece of greaseproof paper and a tight-fitting lid. Cook on a **very low heat** for about 15 minutes to sweat and tenderise without colouring. When cooked, remove from the heat and allow to cool completely.
4 To make the meatballs, put the minced pork and chicken, breadcrumbs, egg, chermoula, Parmesan, parsley and marjoram in a large bowl along with the cooled onions and garlic. Mix and season to taste with salt and pepper. Fry a tiny morsel of the

mixture and taste to check if any further seasoning is required.

5   Form the mixture into 50g balls. This should yield approximately 24 meatballs.

6   Heat the remaining 2 tablespoons of the olive oil in a heavy frying pan set over a medium heat. When the oil is hot, add the meatballs in a single layer, not too tightly packed. Allow them to sit on the heat undisturbed until they colour well before turning them over to colour on all sides. It may be necessary to brown the meatballs in several batches if your pan is not quite large enough. This is important because if you overfill the pan, they will just stew and not develop the delicious flavour from being well coloured at this initial cooking stage. You are not trying to cook the meatballs through at this stage – you are just colouring them.

7   To assemble the dish, scatter the roasted red onions in a large low-sided gratin-type dish and place the meatballs in and around the onions. Add the cherry tomatoes seasoned with a pinch of salt, pepper and sugar. Bring the chicken stock to a simmer, then pour it over. Cover the dish with a dampened sheet of parchment paper.

8   Place in the oven and cook for 1 hour, until the meatballs are cooked through and feel just firm to the touch.

9   Finish the dish with a scattering of the olives, the lemon zest and chopped parsley and serve with grilled sourdough bread.

Chermoula

2 large garlic cloves, peeled and
　　roughly chopped

½–1 medium-hot fresh red chilli,
　　deseeded and chopped

4 tablespoons olive oil

2 tablespoons roughly chopped
　　fresh coriander leaves

1½ teaspoons ground roasted cumin
　　seeds

1½ teaspoons sweet paprika

1 level teaspoon saffron strands

pinch of salt

This is a terrific highly flavoured and spice-laden mixture from North Africa. I love to use it with oily fish such as salmon, mackerel and sardines. It is also great stirred into a bean or lentil soup and folded through couscous. I sometimes smear a little over a grilled steak, lamb or pork chop just before they come off the pan, in which case I like to turn the piece of meat a couple of times on the pan to expose the chermoula to the heat and slightly caramelise it. Lemon wedges and coriander and mint leaves make the perfect garnish for the grilled meats. The mixture holds perfectly in the fridge for two weeks.
Makes 125ml

Place all the ingredients in a food processor and blend to a smooth purée. Taste and correct the seasoning. Transfer to a covered container such as a jam jar and refrigerate until needed.

Grilled Sourdough Bread

4 slices of best-quality
   sourdough bread
1 garlic clove, peeled and cut in half
sea salt
best-quality extra virgin olive oil

Grilled bread can be a revelation. Sourdough bread, olive oil, garlic and sea salt are all that are needed for the simplest version of this dish. However, the quality of each of these four ingredients must be beyond reproach if you are to have one of 'those' food moments.

Carefully chosen toppings can also be smeared on the bread after it has been grilled. If you choose to add a topping, be uncompromisingly seasonal in your choice.

Dark and broody cavolo nero in January, cooked until soft and comforting, can be followed in February by the late shoots on Brussels sprout or broccoli plants, also cooked until soft.

March will bring exciting spring possibilities like wild garlic leaves and their flowers, while late in the month a super treat would be grilled asparagus or sea kale.

April might provide the first tender leaves of mint to pair with a crumbly ewe's milk cheese.

In May you can cook and crush broad beans, melt their leaves in a little hot butter and add a little of the new garlic.

Small beets can be peeled and grated in June and seasoned with a few drops of vino cotto or balsamic vinegar.

The choices in July, August and September won't test you too much, as the possibilities are almost boundless: courgettes, tomatoes, summer greens, peppers, peas, beans, and so on.

*October and November should feature wild mushrooms and some of your dried summer beans like cannellini and borlotti, and of course the first of the new season olive oil. If all else fails in December, don't forget fresh rosemary – simple but rewarding. **Serves 4***

1 Choose a heavy-bottomed cast iron grill pan to cook the bread on. Heat the grill pan until very hot, then add the dry bread and grill on both sides, allowing lots of richly toasted colour to develop. You want the bread to be crisp on the outside but still tender in the middle. Don't allow the bread to cook until it is crisp and brittle all the way through.

2 Remove the bread from the pan and rub **one side only** with the halved garlic clove, but no more than a couple of gentle swipes. Season with a little sea salt. Drizzle generously with olive oil and cut the bread into manageable-sized pieces, making sure each piece of bread has a generous piece of the crust attached. Serve immediately.

Caramel Meringue with Green Gooseberries, Elderflower, Butter-scotch Sauce and Almond Praline

200g demerara sugar

100g egg whites

Filling

400g fresh or frozen gooseberries,
    topped and tailed

50g demerera sugar

2 tablespoons cold water

4 elderflower heads (optional)

2 tablespoons elderflower cordial

250ml cream, softly whipped

To serve

2–4 tablespoons butterscotch sauce
    (page 21)

2–3 tablespoons coarsely ground
    almond praline (page 22)

The gooseberry season is relatively short and I always freeze a few bags to use when there is no fresh fruit available. I like to use the bitter, hard, bright green berries rather than some of the more blushed and sweeter varieties that arrive later in the season. The frozen berries poach really well, but the key is to cook them until they are tender and about to collapse.
Serves 8–10

1 Preheat the oven to 150°C.
2 Place the demerara sugar and egg whites in a spotlessly clean bowl of an electric mixer and **beat until very stiff**. This will take **at least 10 minutes** and sometimes longer. The mixture should hold really sharp peaks and be very firm, to the point that you should have no hesitation about turning the bowl upside down in the knowledge that the meringue won't fall out.
3 While the meringue is beating, use a pencil to draw a 30cm circle on a sheet of non-stick baking paper. Place the paper on a baking sheet, pencil mark side down.
4 As soon as the meringue is stiff and ready, use a large spoon or palate knife to spread it out in a circle in an even layer on the paper. I sometimes pipe a pretty raised edge to the meringue using a large star-shaped nose in a piping bag. The raised edge helps to hold the cream and gooseberries in place when the cooked meringue is filled and ready for serving. Place the meringue in the oven and bake for about 1 hour. You will know the meringue is cooked when it lifts off the paper with no resistance at all. Turn off the oven but leave the meringue in the oven with the door ajar and allow to cool completely.

5 Place the gooseberries, sugar, cold water and elderflower heads (if using) in a small saucepan, cover and set over a gentle heat. Stir occasionally and bring to a simmer. Continue to simmer gently until the **berries are tender** – indeed, some may be starting to burst. Remove from the heat and allow to cool completely.

6 To assemble, place the meringue on a large flat serving plate. Mix the elderflower cordial with the softly whipped cream. If necessary, whip the cream a little more, being careful that the cream does not over-whip and become grainy. Spread the whipped cream on the meringue. Strain the gooseberries out of the cooking syrup and scatter over the cream. (Save any excess poaching liquid for making a homemade lemonade.) Drizzle with the butterscotch sauce and finally sprinkle with the praline powder. If it is elderflower season, I usually decorate the entire dish with a few elderflower heads – so pretty.

7 The meringue can be served immediately or chilled for a couple of hours.

Butterscotch Sauce

275g golden syrup

175g soft dark brown
   Barbados sugar

110g granulated sugar

110g butter

225ml cream

½ teaspoon vanilla extract

Butterscotch sauce is so easy to make and a great thing to have in the fridge to serve with meringues and ice cream. It is also good on thin, crisp apple tarts with a few roasted and chopped pecan nuts or almond praline thrown in for good measure.
Serves 6–8

1　Put the golden syrup, sugars and butter in a heavy-bottomed saucepan and melt gently **over a low heat**, then simmer for about 5 minutes. Remove from the heat and gradually stir in the cream and vanilla. Return to the heat and stir for 2–3 minutes, until all the sugar has dissolved and the sauce is absolutely smooth.

2　Allow to cool, then store in the fridge. The sauce will keep for several months. It will thicken as it chills, so it will probably need to be reheated gently when using at a later stage.

Almond Praline

110g granulated sugar
110g unskinned almonds

Praline powder, ground fine or coarse, has a nutty, caramel flavour and is an essential item in the pastry kitchen. It is used in ice creams, mousses, soufflés, cakes, icings, sweet sauces, biscuits and creams. It can be sprinkled over seasonal berries or scattered over peaches or nectarines before or after roasting. I sometimes just fold it into softly whipped cream to serve with a chocolate cake or pudding. Its uses are too varied to list them all.

Many of the same rules apply here as when you are making caramel. The sugar is cooked with the nuts to a deep chestnut colour, although this time without any water. High temperatures are achieved, which calls for caution for yourself and any others who may be in the kitchen when you are preparing this recipe.

Unskinned almonds have more flavour than the skinned variety. **Makes 220g**

1 Line a baking sheet or tray with non-stick baking paper or a heatproof non-stick baking mat or grease with a light brushing of a bland oil, such as sunflower.
2 Put the sugar and almonds in a **heavy-bottomed**, low-sided saucepan and set on a **medium heat**. The sugar will slowly heat up, melt and start to caramelise. This will not happen evenly, so you will have to use a wooden spoon to gently push the almonds around the pot as the sugar caramelises. The almonds will start to make a cracking sound as they roast in the sugar. When all the sugar is a rich **chestnut colour**, which should take about 10 minutes, quickly coat the nuts in the caramel and **immediately turn them out onto the prepared baking sheet**. Do not touch the mixture with your bare hands under any circumstances, as the caramel will be molten and lava like. If you wish to draw a few individual almonds aside from the bulk of it to be used as a decoration, do it now with the aid of a fork before the mixture sets. Allow to **cool completely** and set into a solid slab.

3 Break the slab of praline into small coarse pieces and grind a few pieces at a time to the powder consistency of your choice in a food processor. I use the **pulse button** so that I can control the size of the grind more accurately. It is also worth saying that the sound of the praline being ground is very loud and you may think that you will damage your machine, but I have ground a lot of praline in my time and have never found this to be the case.

4 Store in a sealed container in a cool, dry place for several weeks.

Hazelnut Praline

110g unskinned hazelnuts

110g granulated sugar

Like almonds, hazelnuts bought with their skins still attached will have more flavour than skinned ones. **Makes 220g**

1 Preheat the oven to 180°C.
2 Place the hazelnuts on a baking tray and roast in the oven for about 15 minutes, until the skins are starting to lift and flake and the nuts are golden brown. Remove the tray from the oven and allow the nuts to cool. Place the cold nuts in a clean kitchen towel, gather up the edges of the towel and rub the base of the towel on the palm of your hand to loosen the skins as much as possible. You will not get every last piece of skin off, but that's fine.
3 Proceed to cook the skinned hazelnuts and sugar as for the almond praline recipe on page 22.

I love the little shrimp that we get by the coast in Cork and wish they were more widely available around the country, though as with all fish nowadays I do worry about the stocks and the management of them. In any case, they are as good as if not better than any shrimp I have had anywhere else in the world and I feel very lucky to be able to get them for a few months each year. When the season ends, I am happy for the little beauties to be left alone to breed and restock and for them to reappear in due course. When cooked, the grey shrimp turn a glorious coral colour, and though they are a bit of a fiddle to peel, they are worth every bit of the effort. This potted shrimp recipe introduces chilli, coriander and smoked paprika to a rather traditional preparation and illustrates the versatility of the flavour of these undervalued fish.

Speaking of treats, is there a greater one than the first taste of sweet, mild spring lamb of the year? In my house this has always been an Easter Sunday treat and prompts a reflective moment of thanks for what the beautiful soil under our feet in this highly fertile country produces for our delectation. When the lamb is this delicate, I resist the temptation to add any further flavour to the succulent meat and instead I concentrate on seasonal accompaniments that will gild rather than overpower that delicacy. A mint-flecked hollandaise is not traditional but is undeniably delicious with the lamb. A mixture of the best of the new season vegetables makes the celebration of the season even greater.

This meal concludes with my version of an Italian classic, cassata, but this cake can be served at any time of the year. I love a few rose petals as the final beautiful and edible decoration on the cake and will be seen looking at the roses in my garden rather anxiously in the weeks before Easter in the hope of a few early buds expressly for that purpose. If you have eaten this cake previously and been underwhelmed by it, as I have, I hope this version will change your view of it.

Both the potted shrimp and the cake can be prepared in advance, which adds to the practical nature of getting this meal to the table.

Potted Shrimp with Chilli, Garlic and Coriander

80–100g butter

110g cooked and peeled shrimp

1 garlic clove, peeled and crushed
  to a paste

1 fresh red chilli, deseeded and
  finely chopped

1 tablespoon chopped fresh
  coriander

lemon juice and zest, to taste

pinch of smoked paprika

sea salt and freshly ground
  black pepper

Potted shrimp are quite simple to make and will keep for several days in the fridge. I like this version, which adds a bit of spice to a traditional preparation. The shrimp can be replaced with cooked lobster, prawns or crayfish, all of which are delicious in this recipe.

Serve with toast, hot bread, grilled sourdough bread (page 16) or Irish brown or white soda bread, lemon wedges and perhaps a little salad of watercress dressed with olive oil and lemon juice. **Serves 6**

1 Melt the butter in a pan and allow to bubble. Add the shrimp, garlic and chilli and **simmer very gently at a bare bubble** for 4 minutes. Allow to cool for about 10 minutes, until the shrimp are at **room temperature**, then add the chopped fresh coriander. Add lemon juice and zest, paprika, salt and pepper to taste. It should taste slightly piquant at this point. Fill into a large pot or individual ones. I like to use a flatter dish rather than the traditional deep pot. Garnish with a whole shrimp if you wish. Chill in the fridge.

2 I like to remove the potted shrimp from the fridge about **15 minutes before serving** so that they are not too cold and solid when they get to the table.

Roast Leg of Spring Lamb with Mint Hollandaise Sauce

1 x 2.7kg leg of spring lamb
sea salt and freshly ground
    black pepper
500ml chicken stock (page 257)
20g butter

To serve
a tangle of spring vegetables
    (page 35)
boiled new potatoes (page 38)
mint hollandaise sauce (page 34)

Spring lamb is a treat, albeit an expensive one, and in my home it is the centrepiece of Easter Sunday lunch. If it is spring lamb with its mild, sweet flavour that you want, make sure to stress the word 'spring' to your butcher. Give plenty of notice with your order out of consideration to your butcher and you will be rewarded for your forward thinking. These lambs are born before or around Christmas, mainly milk fed with a little clover pasture to boot, and are ready for the Easter table. In my opinion it needs nothing added to its thin skin other than salt and pepper to make it into one of the most memorable meals of the year. The spices and stronger herbs associated with lamb are more appropriate with the stronger-tasting meat later in the year.

The most traditional and still one of the best accompaniments for the meat is a classic thin mint sauce, but here I am suggesting a light mint-flavoured hollandaise sauce, which enhances rather than overpowers the flavour of the meat.
Serves 8

1 Preheat the oven to 180°C.
2 Put the lamb in a roasting tin and season with salt and pepper. Place in the oven and roast for 1 hour 10 minutes for pink, 1 hour 20 minutes for medium or 1 hour 30 minutes for well done. Baste the meat with the small amount of fat and cooking juices that gather on the bottom of the roasting tin several times during the cooking.
3 Remove the lamb from the oven and **reduce the temperature to 100°C**. Return the lamb to the warm oven on a platter to rest for at least 15 minutes.
4 While the lamb is resting, make the gravy. Degrease the roasting tray by pouring the liquid into a Pyrex jug, then place the jug in the freezer. Some of the meat juices will be mixed with fat, and as it sits and chills, the fat will rise to the surface and the dark-coloured juices will be visible at the bottom. The fat can be removed and discarded and these juices can be added to the gravy later.

5 Place the roasting tin on a low heat and pour in the chicken stock to deglaze the tin. Whisk vigorously to encourage the caramelised meat juices on the bottom of the roasting tin to dissolve into the stock. Add a pinch of salt and pepper and bring up to a simmer. Strain the gravy through a sieve into a small saucepan and bring back to a simmer. Lift the fat off the chilled meat juices and add the juices to the gravy. Taste to check the flavour. If it tastes a little light, allow it to continue simmering for a few minutes longer so that it reduces and concentrates the flavour. You will have less gravy, but more flavour. Taste again and if you are happy with it now, add the butter and gently whisk it into the sauce at a simmer. As soon as the butter has all been incorporated, remove the gravy from the heat for reheating when needed.

6 Serve the lamb on a hot platter with the **bubbling hot** gravy, spring vegetables and boiled new potatoes and pass the mint hollandaise sauce separately.

Mint Hollandaise Sauce

2 egg yolks

1 tablespoon water

100g butter, cut into 1cm dice

2 teaspoons lemon juice

1–2 tablespoons finely chopped
fresh mint leaves (**chop just
before adding to the sauce**)

*This classic sauce still has its place in my kitchen. All you need
are good eggs and butter and a little lemon juice to sharpen
and you have one of the most useful and delicious of sauces
for serving with fish, fine vegetables such as asparagus and sea
kale and in this case with mild spring lamb. I always chop the
mint just before adding it to the sauce at the last minute. If
you chop the mint ahead of time and allow it to sit at room
temperature or in the fridge, it will oxidise and become bitter.
Serves 6–8*

1 Put the egg yolks and water in a small low-sided
   heavy-bottomed saucepan and whisk well. Put
   on a **low heat** and add the butter three or four
   cubes at a time. Whisk continuously and the butter
   will gradually melt and emulsify into the egg yolks
   and start forming a sauce. Continue whisking and
   adding the butter when the previous additions have
   melted in. **Your only enemy here is too much
   heat**, so keep the heat gentle and if necessary slip
   the saucepan off the heat occasionally if you think
   it is getting too hot. Too much heat will scramble
   the eggs. The side of the saucepan should never at
   any stage of the cooking be too hot for you to touch
   it quickly with your bare fingers. If the sauce shows
   signs of scrambling, add 1 dessertspoon of cold water
   and keep whisking. When all the butter has been
   added, **remove the pan from the heat** and whisk
   in the lemon juice.

2 Decant the sauce into a sauceboat and place it in a
   saucepan of warm tap water, **not on the heat**. The
   sauce, which is served warm rather than hot, will
   keep perfectly for 1 hour. If you find it has cooled
   too much on you, replace the water in the saucepan
   with hand-hot water and stir 1 dessertspoon of
   warm water into the sauce.

3 Just before you are ready to serve, stir the mint into
   the hollandaise sauce.

A Tangle of Spring Vegetables

16 small spring carrots

16 baby beetroot, no bigger than
a golf ball

16 spring onions

16 asparagus spears

16 chard leaves

extra virgin olive oil

sea salt and freshly ground
black pepper

lemon juice

This dish is a mixture of spring vegetables, which pairs beautifully with the spring lamb and indeed most other meats, poultry and fish. The use of the word 'tangle' in the title may cause a few raised eyebrows, but the cooked vegetables are in fact tangled together in a gentle knot, so I am happy that the word is entirely appropriate. I have borrowed it from my Australian friend Skye Gyngell, who cooks some of the most delicious, heavenly food I have ever eaten and with whom I cooked this dish for the first time on the beautiful Isle of Bute off the western coast of Scotland, a precious memory of a glorious time.

These vegetables also make a delicious lunch or supper dish when a coarse grating of Parmesan is added at the very last minute and a soft poached egg and a couple of anchovies are popped on top – with some good bread, a simple but perfect meal. **Serves 8**

1. Preheat the oven to 200°C.
2. Wash or scrub the carrots and beets, leaving 2cm of the stalk attached. Trim the spring onions and rinse them too if necessary. Snap off the tough bottoms of the asparagus spears and economically peel off about 5cm of the remaining tougher skin. Remove the white stalk from the chard leaves and cut them into 3cm pieces at an angle for a more beautiful-looking presentation. Pull the chard leaves into pieces about the size of your hand.
3. Toss the carrots and beets in 2 tablespoons of olive oil and season with salt and pepper. Place on a roasting tray in a single layer and roast in the oven for 15 minutes. After 15 minutes of cooking, add the spring onions to the roasting tray and return to the oven to cook for 5 minutes more.

4 Bring a saucepan of water to the boil, season with salt and add the asparagus. Cook for about 6 minutes, until tender. Remove from the water with a slotted spoon and lay out flat in a single layer to cool slightly. Add the chard stalks to the same boiling water and cook for about 6 minutes before adding the leaves and cooking for a further 3 minutes. Strain and spread out alongside the asparagus to also cool slightly. **Reserve 100ml of the vegetable cooking water.**

5 When all the vegetables are slightly cooled **but still warm**, dress them with olive oil and lemon juice while gently mixing them together. Taste and correct the seasoning. They can be served straight away or reheated later.

6 If I am reheating the vegetables later, I use some of the reserved cooking water to help to prevent them from sticking. Place a wide sauté pan or low-sided saucepan on a medium heat. Add a few tablespoons of the cooking water and bring to a simmer. Add the vegetables and **gently toss them until heated through**. I prefer to serve these vegetables quite hot rather than red hot, as I find that if the heat is too intense, some of the flavour is lost.

Boiled New Potatoes

900g new potatoes, scrubbed

fine sea salt, for cooking the
    potatoes

1 sprig of fresh mint (optional)

butter, to serve

Maldon sea salt, to serve

Most Irish people eagerly await the arrival of the new potato crop. By the time they appear, the main season potatoes will be getting a bit tired and the delicacy of flavour of the new arrivals suits the new spring flavours of lamb, asparagus, and so on.

With new potatoes, freshness is vital. The other key factor is that the potatoes have not been washed before you buy them, as the flavour and texture of the potatoes deteriorate rapidly when the thin, delicate skin is removed.

*The sprig of mint here is optional, but it adds a delicate flavour to the earliest new potatoes. New potatoes need to be served as soon as possible after cooking. **Serves 4–6***

1. Put the potatoes in a saucepan of **boiling water** that they fit snugly into. Add a couple of large pinches of fine salt and the mint (if using). The water should taste quite salty. Cover the pot and cook at a **steady boil for 10 minutes. Strain off most of the water, leaving just 2cm of water in the saucepan, and replace the lid.** Continue cooking at a steady simmer until the potatoes are tender. They will now mostly be cooking in steam. Keep an eye on the saucepan to check that all of the remaining water does not evaporate. The fresher the potatoes, the more quickly they will cook. The size of the potatoes is also a determining factor in the cooking time. Test after a further 10 minutes to see if they are tender – a skewer should pierce them easily and with no resistance.

2. Serve as soon as possible after cooking with Irish butter and sea salt.

Jacket Potatoes

We sometimes forget how good a simple main
season boiled potato cooked in its jacket can be.
The potatoes can be cooked in exactly the same way
as the new potatoes, except I like to start them in cold
water rather than boiling water and the mint can be
omitted. If the potatoes are floury, a knob of butter
makes the perfect sauce and a pinch of sea salt the
perfect seasoning.

Sicilian Cassata

Genoise sponge

4 eggs

110g caster sugar

110g plain flour, sieved, plus extra for
dusting the cake tin

50g butter, melted and cooled, plus
extra for greasing

½ teaspoon vanilla extract

Almond and pistachio paste

100g ground almonds

100g green pistachios

110g caster sugar

2 tablespoons beaten egg

1 drop of almond extract (optional)

Ricotta filling

200g ricotta

50g candied orange peel,
finely diced

1 tablespoon lemon juice

2 teaspoons caster sugar

Apricot glaze

2 tablespoons apricot jam

1 tablespoon lemon juice

To decorate

24 pistachios, finely diced

candied peel

small scented rose petals

lemon geranium leaves (optional)

This is my version of the well-known Sicilian cake. It is always a bit risky for a cook to take a classic recipe and give it a few twists and turns. It is only a worthwhile exercise if you believe your changes are at least as good as the original version. I say with a degree of modesty that I think this interpretation is really good and I am delighted with it. It is a lovely end to this spring meal, when a few fresh rose petals are available for the final flourish on top, but I would be happy to see it in any season. I think it would make a heavenly light summer wedding cake. **Serves 8**

1 Preheat the oven to 180°C.

2 Brush the inside of a 23cm springform cake tin with melted butter and line the base with a circle of non-stick baking paper to fit exactly. Dust the sides of the tin lightly with flour, discarding the excess by tapping the upturned tin on your countertop.

3 Put the eggs in the bowl of a stand mixer fitted with the whisk attachment. Whisk the eggs for a few seconds, then add the caster sugar in gradually in a stream. Continue whisking on a high speed for about 10 minutes, until the mixture has **doubled in volume** and is light and thick enough to make a distinct figure of 8 when the whisk is lifted.

4 Fold the flour into the egg mixture in three batches, **folding each batch as lightly as possible** with a long-handled spatula. Just after you have folded in the last batch, pour the melted butter and vanilla extract around the side of the bowl and fold them in quickly and gently, as the batter will lose volume as soon as the butter is added.

5 Pour the batter into the prepared tin, gently smooth the surface and bake in the oven for 30–35 minutes, until the cake shrinks very slightly from the sides of the tin and the top springs back when lightly pressed.

Remove from the oven and place the tin on a wire rack to relax for 10 minutes before removing the cake from the tin. Place the cake on the wire rack, paper side down, and leave to cool completely.

6 To make the paste, place the almonds and pistachios in a food processor and process until fine. Tip out into a bowl and add the sugar, beaten egg and almond extract (if using). Mix with a wooden spoon or your hands until it **comes together into a smooth paste**.

7 Roll the paste into a 23cm circle that will exactly fit and cover the top of the cake. It may be necessary to use a little ground almonds to prevent the paste from sticking as you roll it. I use the cake tin as a template.

8 Gently mix all the ricotta filling ingredients together until well combined.

9 Heat the apricot jam and lemon juice to a bare simmer in a small saucepan set over a low heat and stir occasionally. Sieve into a small bowl.

10 Once the cake has cooled completely, remove the paper and carefully cut it in half horizontally. Fill with the ricotta mixture and sandwich the two halves together.

11 Brush the top of the cake with the apricot glaze. Place the circle of almond and pistachio paste on top and brush **the whole cake**, including the paste-covered top, with the remaining glaze.

12 Decorate the top of the cake with pistachios, candied peel and small scented rose petals and lemon geranium leaves. Serve at room temperature.

I hope I will be forgiven for including tuna in the starter of this meat-free meal, as it does have a somewhat meaty texture and robust flavour. Tuna is not one of the fish we think of as part of the Irish catch, but there is a lot of this marvellous ingredient being landed here and it is that Irish landed fish I want when I make this elegant dish. The dressing is spiky but well balanced and the crisp, peppery radishes and spring onions add a good texture and look quite pretty scattered over the thinly sliced raw fish. Mackerel makes an excellent substitute for the tuna and I regularly use that in this dish. As with any fish dish, but especially a raw fish dish, the freshness of the fish is paramount to achieve a sweet, untainted flavour.

The technique for the tart in this meal really excites me as a useful one for all cooks. The crisp pastry base and low sides look great and a myriad of ingredients, either savoury or sweet, will cook beautifully in this pastry vehicle. The elephant in this room, of course, is the pastry. I have included the recipe for homemade puff pastry and I promise you that it is not the torturous procedure it is often made out to be. In fact, I know of few kitchen tasks that give as much reward for so little effort as puff pastry does. The combination of Irish ricotta, onions, mushrooms and thyme is deeply savoury and satisfying. A salad of mixed leaves with a dressing made with good olive oil is all that is needed to complete the main course.

I have always loved prunes, but I know that some are less enamoured with the dried plums, which have an important role to play in both the sweet and savoury kitchen. Here they are tender and plumped up after a good soak in leaf tea and they pair perfectly with the jasmine and lemon in the parfait. Poached gooseberries or rhubarb would be a good seasonal alternative to the prunes. In fact, the parfait can be made at any time of year and respond to the accompanying seasonal fruit accordingly.

Sashimi of Tuna with Crisped Radishes and Spring Onions

50g radishes, very thinly sliced

4 spring onions, very thinly sliced at
    an angle

200g fresh tuna fillet or 4 large
    mackerel fillets

1 tablespoon sesame oil

sea salt and freshly ground black
    pepper

4 tablespoons micro greens or very
    tiny salad leaves, fresh coriander
    leaves and flowers, chopped fresh
    chives and chive flowers

Dressing

70g very finely chopped onion

2 tablespoons soy sauce

2 tablespoons rice vinegar

1 dessertspoon water

1 tablespoon grapeseed oil

1 tablespoon sesame oil

1 teaspoon caster sugar

¼ teaspoon dry mustard powder

sea salt and freshly ground
    black pepper

Occasionally I can get tuna that has been caught in Irish waters, and when I do, this is one of my favourite ways to serve the fish. Failing the tuna, fat mackerel fillets are also excellent. It is crucial when sealing or searing the fish to just barely do that and not to overcook it – all you want is a thin line of external colour. **Serves 4**

1. First soak the sliced radishes and spring onions in a bowl of ice water for 30 minutes to crisp up.
2. To prepare the tuna, heat a dry, heavy-bottomed, non-stick frying pan or a cast iron grill until very hot. Rub the tuna fillet all over with the tablespoon of sesame oil and season with sea salt and black pepper. Sear the tuna very quickly on all sides to achieve a blanched or very pale golden line of colour on the outside of the fish. **The tuna should spend no more than 2 minutes in the pan.** Remove the tuna from the pan immediately, allow to cool slightly and chill.
3. If using mackerel, paint the flesh side of the fillet with the sesame oil and sear for a matter of seconds on a hot non-stick pan. Remove and chill.
4. Combine all the dressing ingredients, mixing well to blend the oils, vinegar and soy sauce. Taste and correct the seasoning. Keep chilled until ready to use.
5. To serve, spread 1 tablespoon of the dressing on each of four plates. With a very sharp knife, cut the seared tuna very thinly into slices about 3mm thick and divide between the plates in a single layer. If using mackerel, cut it into slices 3mm thick straight down through the flesh and skin.
6. Season the fish with a little more sea salt and freshly ground black pepper and drizzle a little of the remaining dressing over the fish. Garnish the plates with the drained and dried radishes and spring onions, micro greens, herbs and flowers and serve immediately.

Tart of Macroom Buffalo Ricotta with Roasted Red Onions, Mushrooms, Thyme and Marjoram

250g puff pastry (page 256)

2 medium red onions, peeled and each onion cut into 8 even-sized wedges

2 tablespoons + 2 teaspoons extra virgin olive oil

2 large sprigs of fresh thyme

sea salt and freshly ground black pepper

100g buffalo or sheep's milk ricotta

25g Parmesan, grated

½ teaspoon fresh thyme leaves

1 large flat mushroom

2 teaspoons fresh marjoram leaves

To serve

salad of mixed leaves (page 49)

I am delighted to be able to use Irish ricotta that comes from Macroom in County Cork, where the buffalos that produce the milk for the cheese are happily grazing on Irish grass. I find these sort of sustainable developments in Irish food production quite thrilling and I congratulate all involved who had the vision and energy to run with an idea that may have sounded harebrained to many.

The tart can be served as a starter or as a main course and I always serve a salad of mixed leaves with a simple olive oil dressing to accompany it. The quality of the puff pastry you are using is really important for a fresh-tasting result that isn't greasy. I always make my own puff pastry and freeze a few pieces so that I have it to hand when I need it. If you are buying puff pastry, make sure it is made with butter. The technique used here for creating a tart using puff pastry is one that can be repeated over and over again with other vegetables and fruit.

The mushroom in the recipe is one of those big flat mature mushrooms that has dark brown gills rather than the smaller ones with pink gills. The more deeply flavoured mushroom that I favour here stands up well to the robust flavour of the roasted onions and pairs well with the delicate ricotta. **Serves 4**

1 Preheat the oven to 200°C. Line a baking sheet with non-stick baking paper.

2 Roll the pastry out and cut into a neat 22cm circle, saving the pastry trimmings for another day. Place on the lined baking sheet. To achieve a rim on the cooked tart, cut another circle 1cm in from the edge of the pastry. Your knife should pierce the pastry about **1mm** deep and should be an obvious cut, not just a mark. This 1cm rim will be the risen edge of the cooked tart and will hold the vegetables in place.

3 Now pierce the pastry **inside** the 1cm rim all over with a normal table fork, making sure you feel the tines of the fork hitting the baking sheet. **Do not pierce outside of the 1cm rim with your fork.** The somewhat alarming holes you have created with the fork in the bottom of the pastry will close and reseal when it cooks. Chill the pastry until you are ready to assemble the tart.

4 Toss the onions in 2 tablespoons of the olive oil, add the thyme sprigs and season with salt and pepper. Tip into a roasting tray and cook in the oven for 30 minutes, until tender. Cool completely.

5 Mix the ricotta with the Parmesan, thyme leaves and the remaining 2 teaspoons of olive oil and season with salt and pepper.

6 To assemble the tart, spread the ricotta mixture over the base, **making sure not to go onto the pastry rim**. Arrange the roasted onions on top. Cut the mushroom into slices 1cm thick and place cap side down, stalk side up, in a circle on top of the onions. Season the mushroom slices. If the thyme sprigs still look reasonably respectable, I pop those on top as well as I love their roasted appearance.

7 Cook in the oven for 30 minutes, until the pastry is crisp and cooked through. Add a final few grains of sea salt and the marjoram leaves and serve as soon as possible.

Salad of Mixed Leaves

4 large handfuls of mixed leaves,
carefully **washed and dried**, and
comprised of a mixture of some
of the following;

butterhead lettuce, oakleaf,
mustard leaves, mizuna, mibuna

lambs lettuce, torn into little
bunches or individual leaves

radicchio and chicory leaves, torn
into bite-sized pieces

Brussels sprouts, leaves separated
or finely shredded

cabbage leaves, very finely
shredded across the grain

kale leaves, destalked and pulled
into small bite-sized pieces

watercress or landcress, separated
into individual sprigs or leaves

cavolo nero leaves, the tiniest
ones left whole or larger
ones destalked and torn into
bite-sized pieces

fresh chives and parsley, coarsely
chopped

Dressing

¼ teaspoon Dijon mustard

¼ teaspoon honey (optional)

sea salt and freshly ground black
pepper

1 tablespoon white or red wine
vinegar

4 tablespoons extra virgin olive oil

A salad of mixed seasonal leaves is an essential part of my diet, not just as a healthy plate of food, but also as the perfect accompaniment to many dishes. A carefully composed selection of leaves with a dressing made with good-quality oil and vinegar has a light and refreshing effect on the diner, and whether served as a side dish or as a single course, it is a cornerstone of many meals in my house. The leaves, either cultivated or foraged, can be bolstered with edible flowers or less likely salad ingredients such as shaved Brussels sprouts, tiny bits of kale or even very finely shredded green cabbage.

I only use the optional honey in the recipe if I have a particularly bitter selection of leaves, such as radicchio, curly endive or chicory. **Serves 4**

1 To make the dressing, place the mustard, honey (if using) and a pinch of salt and pepper in a small bowl. Add the vinegar and whisk in the olive oil in a steady stream. Taste and correct the seasoning.

2 To assemble the salad, place the leaves in a very large bowl. I always use a bowl that looks ridiculously big for the task to ensure I can lift and toss the leaves in the dressing with ease and not crush and bruise them. Whisk the dressing again to make sure the oil and vinegar are properly mixed and add just enough dressing to the leaves to lightly coat them. Lift up the leaves with your fingers open wide to encourage the dressing to coat them evenly. Taste to see if a little extra salt is needed. Transfer to a clean bowl or plates and serve immediately.

Jasmine Tea and Lemon Parfait with Tea-Soaked Prunes

150g caster sugar

100ml water

1 tablespoon jasmine tea leaves

6 egg yolks

2 tablespoons lemon juice

450ml cream, whipped to soft peaks

zest of 1 lemon

To serve

jasmine tea-soaked prunes (page 52)

softly whipped cream

*I like the subtle flavour of jasmine in this dish. The tender frozen parfait can be served on its own, but it pairs well with the tea-soaked prunes. In summer I also serve this with a fruit salad (page 122) or with a simple bowl of really ripe strawberries. Other highly scented tea leaves, such as lapsang souchong or Earl Grey black tea with bergamot, could replace the jasmine tea leaves with equally delicious results. **Serves** 10*

1 Line a 25cm x 10cm loaf tin or terrine with cling film and chill.

2 Place the sugar and water in a small saucepan and bring to the boil. Remove from the heat and add the tea leaves. Leave to steep and infuse for 10 minutes. **Strain the tea out of the syrup**, pressing the leaves well to extract all the flavour.

3 Place the egg yolks in a mixing bowl and whisk to a light, fluffy mousse. Bring the strained syrup back to the boil and pour it onto the egg yolks in a steady stream, whisking all the time. Add the lemon juice and continue beating until the mixture is a light and airy mousse and holds a light figure of 8 with the whisk. This can take up to 10 minutes to achieve. Chill for 5 minutes.

4 Gently fold in the whipped cream and lemon zest. Pour into the lined tin and freeze until set.

5 To serve the parfait, turn it out of the tin, remove the cling film and cut it into slices 2cm thick. Serve with a few tea-soaked prunes, a little of the prune syrup and some softly whipped cream on the side.

Jasmine Tea-Soaked Prunes

500g prunes (with stones in)

500ml water

1 tablespoon jasmine tea leaves

40g caster sugar

6 thin strips of orange rind

½ vanilla pod

*Prunes are a bit controversial, with as many haters as lovers. I have always enjoyed them, whether in a savoury situation rolled into a loin of roast pork or as a soft and unctuous offering at the end of a meal. They can absorb many different flavours and here the scented jasmine tea matches perfectly with the dried fruit. If you have any of these left over, they make a delicious simple dessert or breakfast with a spoonful of thick natural yogurt. I like the cooking juices to be slightly thickened to coat the prunes in a glistening syrup. **Serves 8–10***

1 Place the prunes in a small saucepan. Bring the water to a boil and pour it over the tea leaves in a separate bowl and allow to infuse for 5 minutes. **Strain the jasmine tea through a sieve** over the prunes and add the sugar, orange rind and vanilla pod. Place on a gentle heat and bring to a simmer. Immediately remove from the heat and allow to cool completely. Cover and chill for at least 12 hours or ideally overnight.

2 The next day, strain the liquid off the prunes and place in a low-sided saucepan. Bring to a simmer and reduce by half, until it appears slightly syrupy, but be careful not to overcook or the syrup will become too thick and sticky. Pour the slightly thickened, reduced liquid back over the prunes and they are now ready to serve or can be chilled again. The prunes will now keep in the fridge for a week or longer.

Asparagus spears majestically pushing up through the earth towards the sun is a sight to behold. If we get some warm spring sunshine, you can almost see them stretching and craning towards the light. Often cited as the vegetable that most illustrates the point of seasonal eating, it has a place in my food calendar that will not be changing. Allowing for the vagaries of the weather, I expect to start to see it around the beginning of April and nothing will make me eat it at other times of the year. The season lasts about six weeks, sometimes a little longer, and then it is gone. While it is here I eat as much of it as I can and am happy to wave goodbye to it after the relatively brief but delicious sojourn. I will always eat the first few spears of the year with a mint hollandaise sauce (page 34) or a green sauce (page 57), and when that annual yearning has been sated, I will make this elegant salad. The eggs and olives pair well with the aristocratic vegetable and a few wispy shavings of Parmesan add to the satisfying savoury combination.

Monkfish is a firm-textured, flavoursome white fish. It can be grilled, roasted, pan fried or deep fried and is a favourite choice for a ceviche, where it is 'cooked' by citrus juice rather than heat. It needs a fair bit of trimming to remove the rather tough layers of skin and membrane before the brilliantly white flesh is revealed. The poaching technique used to cook it in this recipe is quick and easy, and with a good eye you will have perfectly cooked fish. I think this is one of the easiest and most successful ways of cooking fish for a large number of people, as you can poach up to 12 main course portions in a medium-sized saucepan, and all in only a few minutes' cooking time. The light, frothy green sauce complements the fish perfectly. Almost any seasonal green vegetable will work here, such as broad beans, and a delicate boiled new potato will complete the picture.

I have included the hazelnut panna cotta here for those who can't countenance getting past Easter without some chocolate, as the sauce that is served with the gently set cream is a chocolate lover's dream. The panna cotta can be made a day ahead and stored, covered, in the fridge. The sauce can also be made ahead but will need a gentle reheating just to loosen the consistency to a pouring sauce rather than to serve it warm. All told, this is a perfect combination of flavours.

Asparagus Mimosa Salad

2 eggs

16–20 fat asparagus spears

16 fat Kalamata olives

20 rocket leaves

12 thin Parmesan shavings or pieces

1 tablespoon finely chopped chives

chive and wild garlic flowers, if
   available

Dressing

1 small garlic clove, peeled and
   crushed to a paste

2 tablespoons extra virgin olive oil

2 tablespoons sunflower oil

1 tablespoon balsamic vinegar

sea salt and freshly ground
   black pepper

This combination of ingredients showcases the asparagus really well. The mimosa in the recipe title refers to the sieved hard-boiled egg yolks, which has a visual effect similar to that of the flowers on a mimosa tree. **Serves 4**

1   Hard-boil the eggs by lowering them gently into a saucepan of **boiling salted water** and cooking them at a boil for exactly 10 minutes. If you don't want the yolk to be completely hard, cook for 9 minutes. The salt in the water seasons the egg and will help to coagulate any white that might seep out of a crack in the shell, hence less leakage. Remove from the saucepan immediately with a slotted spoon and cool under a cold running tap.

2   Remove the shell and cut the hard-boiled eggs in half. Chop the white finely. Pass the yolk through a sieve, using the back of a soup spoon to push the egg through to achieve a mimosa-type effect. **Keep the chopped white and sieved yolk separate.**

3   To prepare the asparagus for cooking, snap off the tough end as close to the end of the spear as possible. Peel the tough skin from the bottom 6cm of each stalk. Try not to be too heavy-handed when peeling the stalks to avoid losing too much of the precious spears and also so as not to spoil the shape.

4   Stone the olives by gently squashing them on a chopping board with the back of a knife and removing the stones. Chop the olive flesh finely and reserve.

5   Whisk all the ingredients for the dressing together, taste and correct the seasoning.

6   Bring 1 litre of water to a boil in a low-sided saucepan. Season with salt and add the prepared asparagus. Poach for about 8 minutes, until perfectly tender but not soft and overcooked. Remove immediately from the cooking water and spread out on a wire rack to drain. Dress the asparagus when the spears have cooled slightly but are **still slightly warm** to help seal in the flavour.

7   To assemble the salad, place the rocket leaves on four large plates, trying to create a circular pattern towards the edge of each plate. Sprinkle the chopped olives inside the circle of leaves and follow with the egg white. Place the asparagus on top of the olives and sprinkle over the egg yolk to create the mimosa effect. Place three Parmesan shavings or pieces on each salad. Finally, sprinkle on the chopped chives and flowers, if available. Serve as soon as possible.

Poached Monkfish with Green Sauce

900g monkfish tails, carefully
    trimmed of skin and membrane
1.1 litres water
2 teaspoons salt

Green sauce
2 eggs
1 tablespoon water
100g cold butter, diced
1 teaspoon chopped fresh chives
1 teaspoon chopped fresh chervil
1 teaspoon chopped fennel fronds
1 teaspoon chopped fresh parsley
lemon juice

To serve
broad beans (page 60)
boiled new potatoes (page 38)
fresh herb sprigs, to garnish

I like the lightness and the almost foamy consistency of this green sauce, which is achieved by the last-minute addition of whisked egg whites. The technique for poaching the monkfish is quick, easy and effective. The short cooking time is crucial, so do be vigilant and don't overcook the fish. **Serves 6**

1   Cut the monkfish tails into 2cm-thick slices, or collops as they are known as, and refrigerate until needed.

2   To make the sauce, separate the eggs and place the yolks in a small low-sided saucepan. Place **one** of the egg whites in a spotlessly clean bowl. Reserve the remaining egg white in the fridge or freezer for another use. Add the tablespoon of water to the yolks and whisk to mix. **Place on a very low heat** and cook for 30 seconds before adding in the butter two or three pieces at a time while whisking constantly. The butter will gradually melt into the sauce and emulsify. Continue to whisk in the butter until it has all been incorporated into a sauce. Be careful during this process to control the heat under the saucepan – **don't allow the pan to become too hot or the eggs will scramble**. If at any stage the sauce starts to look odd, remove the saucepan from the heat, add 1 tablespoon of water and continue to whisk. Once the sauce is done, keep it warm by pushing the saucepan to the back of the stove. Otherwise you can decant the sauce into a Pyrex jug or pottery bowl and sit it into a saucepan of hot water. Do not put the saucepan on the heat. The water can be topped up with hot water to maintain the sauce at a warm but not hot temperature. The sauce will keep perfectly like this for at least an hour.

3 Just before you are ready to cook the fish, whisk the egg white to a firm but not dry peak and fold it into the warm butter sauce along with the chopped herbs and a few drops of lemon juice. The effect should be a light, frothy green sauce.

4 Bring the water to the boil and add the salt. Add the collops of monkfish and **simmer for 4–5 minutes**, until the fish is completely white and no longer opaque. Drain well.

5 To serve, arrange the fish in a warm serving dish or on individual plates. Coat each piece of fish with the sauce, garnish with sprigs of fresh herbs and serve immediately.

Broad Beans

600ml water

sea salt and freshly ground
   black pepper

500g broad beans, weighed after
   removing the beans from their
   pods

10g butter or 1 tablespoon extra
   virgin olive oil

*Broad beans are another of my favourite vegetables. I can happily eat a plate of them on their own with a little melted butter or olive oil and a piece of hot grilled bread (page 16). There is a bit of work involved in the preparation of the beans, but they are worth the effort. Begin by removing the thick, sponge-lined pod to find the pale green beans within. These are cooked and then I always remove the slightly leathery skins to reveal the beautifully green and tender prize. If you are preparing the beans ahead of time, as I often do, keep them well chilled until you are ready to reheat them. I always keep a little of the bean cooking water and then gently toss them in that over a gentle heat to bring them to the temperature I require. **Serves 4–6***

1 Bring the water to a rolling boil, add a good pinch of salt and add the beans. Cook the beans, **uncovered**, for about 5 minutes, by which time you should notice the leathery skin on the beans starting to crack to expose the bright green bean inside. Taste one of the beans to ensure it is tender. If so, strain the beans through a colander, **reserving about 6 tablespoons of cooking water** for reheating the beans later. If you don't mind the skins on the broad beans, you can toss the beans in a little butter or olive oil now and serve them immediately. Unless the beans are really tiny, I prefer to run them under a cold running tap, still in the colander, to stop them from overcooking. Spread them out onto a flat tray to cool. Now pinch the beans out of their skins. Discard the skins, unless there is someone in the kitchen who likes them. The peeled beans can be reheated for serving now or kept cool until later.

2 To reheat the beans, bring the reserved cooking water to a gentle simmer in a small wide saucepan. Add the beans and just warm them through. This will take only a matter of minutes. Broad beans should never be served red hot, as they will overcook and spoil. Finally and quickly, add the butter or oil, a little black pepper and mix. By now the water will have evaporated and the beans will have a light shiny glaze. Taste to check the seasoning and serve immediately in a warm serving dish.

Roast Leg of Spring Lamb with
Mint Hollandaise Sauce, *p30*

Sicilian Cassata, *p41*

A Tangle of Spring
Vegetables, *p35*

Roasted Hazelnut Panna Cotta with Chocolate and Caramel Sauce

100g unskinned hazelnuts

600ml cream

35g caster sugar

½ teaspoon vanilla extract

1½ teaspoons powdered gelatine

2 tablespoons water

To serve

chocolate and caramel sauce
(page 66)

This delicious combination of cream, vanilla, chocolate, caramel and hazelnuts is very good indeed. The set panna cotta and the chocolate sauce will keep perfectly in the fridge for a couple of days, though keep them covered to preserve the delicate flavours. The key to a good panna cotta is that it is just barely set and wobbles as you bring it to the table. If the cream is too set, the delicate and trembling charm of the dish is lost. ***Serves 6–8***

1 Preheat the oven to 200°C.

2 Place the hazelnuts on a roasting tray and roast in the oven for about 15 minutes, until the nuts are roasted to a rich golden colour and the skins are starting to lift. Remove from the oven and allow to cool. Place the nuts in a clean towel and rub off as many of the skins as possible. Discard the skins. Chop the nuts coarsely and add to the cream. **Bring the cream and nuts to a shivering heat and remove from the heat immediately.** Allow to cool completely, then cover and refrigerate for several hours or overnight.

3 The next day, use a sieve to strain the nuts out of the cream, pressing well to extract as much of the cream as possible. **Reserve the nuts for later.** Place the cream in a saucepan and add the sugar and vanilla extract. Place on a low heat to dissolve the sugar. **The cream must not boil** – it should just be shivering on the surface. Remove from the heat and allow to cool, though it does not need to get completely cold.

4 Measure the gelatine into a Pyrex jug or bowl. Add the water and stir very gently to mix. Allow to sit for a few minutes to 'sponge'. This term will become clear when you see the sponge-like appearance of the gelatine. Place the bowl in a saucepan of barely simmering water and allow it to heat to dissolve the gelatine to **a completely clear liquid**.

5 **Pour the cream onto the gelatine** while whisking continuously and mix well.

6 Place the mixture in your serving dish or dishes of choice and refrigerate until set. If you wish to turn out the panna cottas when serving, you will need to oil the receptacles with a tasteless oil such as sunflower or grapeseed before filling.

7 Refrigerate the panna cotta to set, allowing 4 hours or overnight if you wish. Serve the panna cotta with the chocolate and caramel sauce.

Chocolate and Caramel Sauce

225g caster or granulated sugar

250ml cream

150g chocolate (at least 62%
cocoa solids), roughly chopped

1 teaspoon vanilla extract

hazelnuts strained from the cream in
the panna cotta on page 64

This rich and delicious sauce captures the flavour of chocolate and caramel beautifully. **Makes about 15 servings**

1 Place the dry sugar in a deep heavy-bottomed saucepan and cook over a moderate heat until it is a chestnut-coloured caramel. This will take about 8 minutes and you will need to stir the sugar at intervals to encourage it to cook evenly. At stages during the cooking the sugar will look odd and lumpy and you may think it has gone wrong on you. Just keep stirring and at the very last moment before the chestnut colour is achieved, the caramel, as if by magic, will become clear and the little lumps of sugar will dissolve.

2 **As soon as the chestnut caramel has been achieved, immediately pull the saucepan off the heat and add the cream.** Be careful, as it will splutter, so you may need to add the cream by degrees. Stir with a flat-bottomed wooden spoon to encourage the cream and caramel to mix. Some of the caramel may have solidified, so it may be necessary to return the saucepan to a low heat to encourage the caramel to dissolve. Allow to cool for 5 minutes before stirring in the chocolate and vanilla. Stir continuously to melt the chocolate into the sauce.

3 **The strained hazelnuts from the panna cotta recipe may be stirred into the sauce at this point.**

4 The sauce will keep in the fridge for at least a week. It will firm up and will need gentle reheating to liquefy it again for use.

MEAL 5

–

**Scrambled Eggs
with Lobster and Chives**

–

Grilled Sourdough Bread

–

**Duck Leg Curry with
Cider Vinegar**

–

Plain Boiled Rice

–

Peas with Mint

–

**Rhubarb and Blood
Orange Open Tart with
Grenadine Cream**

The scrambled eggs here, enriched with cream and lobster, can be prepared in advance and kept at room temperature for several hours. I sometimes replace the lobster with shrimp or sautéed chanterelle mushrooms when wild mushrooms are in season. Sea kale or asparagus, when in season, are also delicious folded through the eggs. The eggs can be served with toast or hot crisped white bread, but my favourite accompaniment is the grilled sourdough bread on page 16.

The duck curry is full of Indian flavours. I prefer to use duck legs and cook them for plenty of time to ensure a tender texture. Plain boiled rice is perfect with the flavoursome duck and almost any green vegetable will complete the picture. Be generous with the vegetable of choice, as the duck meat is rich and the vegetables will lighten the whole experience. I have suggested peas as they pair beautifully with duck, but any of the broccolis, beans or green cabbage would also be good. The duck curry reheats perfectly, so I would have no hesitation about preparing it in advance. If I am making this later in the year, as I sometimes do, I serve boiled new potatoes (page 38) to replace the rice and they are also delicious with the rich duck.

The tart to finish this meal is a lovely thing and both the pastry and the technique for assembling the tart can be used all the way through the year for open-faced fruit tarts. Rhubarb and blood oranges are a delicious combination. The suggested grenadine cream to serve with the tart is a perfect marriage of flavours with the rhubarb and orange. This tart is at its most delicious when served warm with the chilled flavoured cream.

Scrambled Eggs with Lobster and Chives

225g cooked lobster (see page 262), chopped into 2cm pieces

4 tablespoons cream

8 free-range eggs

sea salt and freshly ground black pepper

25g butter

grilled sourdough bread (page 16), to serve

finely grated zest of 1 lemon

2 tablespoons finely chopped fresh chives

1 tablespoon chive flowers (optional)

This is a delicious combination that can be served as a starter or canapé on grilled bread or melba toast. Shrimp or crayfish could replace the lobster in the recipe. The addition of cream to the cooked eggs prevents the mixture from solidifying, making it an ideal dish to prepare in advance. I hold the cooked mixture at room temperature for a couple of hours and serve it on hot grilled or toasted bread.

*The optional chive flowers make a pretty and delicious garnish, but they could be replaced another time with garlic, kale or fennel flowers. **Serves 4 as a starter or 30 as a canapé***

1 Place the lobster and cream in a small saucepan and gently **heat to a bare simmer**, then remove from the heat.

2 Beat the eggs with a good pinch of salt and pepper.

3 Melt the butter in a small heavy-bottomed saucepan. Add the beaten eggs and cook over a gentle heat, stirring all the time with a flat-bottomed wooden spoon. **When the eggs are just beginning to scramble**, add the lobster and cream and keep cooking for a few more minutes, until the eggs are a creamy consistency. Remove from the heat and transfer from the saucepan to a bowl. The eggs will not set hard like cold scrambled eggs, but will retain their lovely softness. The eggs are best served barely warm but are also good at room temperature.

4 When ready to serve, spread the scrambled eggs over the hot grilled bread. Grate over the lemon zest and finish with a sprinkling of chives and chive flowers (if using). Serve immediately.

Duck Leg Curry with Cider Vinegar

1 tablespoon ground cumin

1 tablespoon ground coriander

1 tablespoon bright red paprika
 (not smoked)

1½ teaspoons garam masala

1 teaspoon ground turmeric

pinch of cayenne pepper

2 teaspoons sunflower oil

8 duck legs, cut to yield 8 thighs and
 8 drumsticks

1 teaspoon brown mustard seeds

¼ teaspoon whole fenugreek seeds

2 medium onions, peeled and
 thinly sliced

15 curry leaves (optional)

6 garlic cloves, peeled and crushed
 to a paste

2 tablespoons finely grated
 fresh ginger

2 ripe tomatoes, peeled
 and chopped

75–100ml apple cider vinegar

1 tablespoon caster sugar

1 teaspoon salt, plus more to taste

To serve

plain boiled rice (page 72) or boiled
 new potatoes (page 38)

peas with mint (page 73)

chopped fresh flat-leaf parsley,
 to garnish

This is a deeply flavoursome dish that reheats perfectly, so it is ideal to prepare ahead for a party or a large family meal. By the time the curry is cooked, the rich, amber-coloured duck fat will have risen to the top of the dish. I always leave that where it is and serve it with the curry. **Serves 4–6**

1 Mix the spices in a small bowl and set aside.

2 Heat the oil in a heavy-bottomed casserole. Dry the duck pieces and place them in the casserole, skin side down, and cook for about 8 minutes, until hazelnut brown. Turn and repeat on the other side, then remove from the casserole. If there is an excessive amount of rendered duck fat at this stage, spoon some of it out and reserve for another use.

3 Add the mustard and fenugreek seeds and allow the mustard to pop, which will only take **a matter of seconds**. Immediately add the sliced onions and curry leaves (if using) and cook for about 10 minutes, until the edges of the onions are lightly browned. Add the garlic and ginger and fry for 1 minute. Add the spices and cook over a gentle heat, stirring all the while, for 30 seconds. Add the tomatoes and cook for 3 minutes. Add the browned duck pieces back to the casserole along with the vinegar, sugar, salt and **enough water to barely cover the duck**, then stir to gently mix.

4 Bring the curry to a simmer and cover the pot. Cook at this **gentle simmer** for 45 minutes. Remove the lid and continue to cook at a simmer for a further 30 minutes, occasionally stirring and scraping the bottom of the casserole. By now the sauce should have reduced and thickened slightly and the duck should be really tender. Taste and correct the seasoning.

5 Ladle the curry into warmed bowls and scatter over the parsley. Serve with plain boiled rice or boiled new potatoes and serve the peas with mint (or the green vegetable of your choice) on the side.

Plain Boiled Rice

2 litres water

1 teaspoon salt

200g basmati rice

a little butter or olive oil

chopped fresh parsley (optional)

This method for cooking rice is very different from the old-fashioned proportion of 1 cup of rice to 2 cups of water. Cooking rice in a lot of water produces an excellent result. The rice remains fluffy and in separate grains and will keep quite happily covered in an oven for half an hour. **Serves 8**

1 Preheat the oven to 140°C.
2 Bring the water to a boil. Add the salt and sprinkle in the rice. Stir gently to separate the grains of rice. Bring back to the boil and cook, uncovered, for 5 minutes. Taste the rice – it should be a little undercooked. Strain through a sieve or colander.
3 Put in a warm serving dish and dot with a few knobs of butter or a drizzle of olive oil. Cover the dish tightly with dampened parchment paper and place in the oven for 15 minutes at least. The rice will finish cooking. Remove the paper to serve. Fluff up with a fork and add a little chopped parsley if you wish.

Peas with Mint

500ml water

sea salt and freshly ground
    black pepper

450g peas

10g butter or 1 tablespoon extra
    virgin olive oil

1 tablespoon finely chopped fresh
    mint leaves (**chop just before
    adding**)

Simple and easy, peas always seem to please. **Serves 4**

Bring the water to a rolling boil and add a good
pinch of salt. Add the peas and cook, uncovered, for
about 5 minutes, until tender. Drain in a sieve or a
colander and put back in the warm saucepan. Add the
butter or olive oil and stir it in gently, then stir in the
frest mint just before serving. Taste and correct the
seasoning, adding a little freshly ground black pepper
if you wish. Serve immediately in a warm serving dish.

Rhubarb and Blood Orange Open Tart with Grenadine Cream

Sour cream pastry

250g plain white flour, plus extra
    for dusting

200g chilled butter, diced

pinch of salt

155g sour or fresh cream

Filling

450g rhubarb, thinly sliced

150g caster sugar, plus a little extra

1 vanilla pod, halved lengthways
    and very finely chopped

2 blood oranges, peeled and cut
    into 5mm slices

a little beaten egg

Grenadine cream

200ml softly whipped cream

2 tablespoons grenadine syrup

The first precious and expensive pale pink (or what I call Chanel pink) rhubarb stalks of the season to appear are sometimes referred to as champagne rhubarb. A lovely name indeed, though somewhat confusing, as there is a variety of rhubarb called champagne, but that is generally not the variety grown for those forced stalks. So I suppose we can accept the use of the word champagne to describe the first forced stalks as a word of celebration for the first fresh fruit of the year, rather than a reference to the variety being grown. The other beautifully coloured fruit that arrives in this part of the world around the same time as the rhubarb is the blood orange, and what a joy that is too. The flesh and juice are a deep blood red colour, and raw, or in this case, cooked, it is a wonderful ingredient. My preferred variety here is the Tarocco, which is revered in Italy. The two early arrivals pair beautifully and this is borne out in this tart. The tart has a rather rustic appearance but is nonetheless quite beautiful.

I suggest serving a grenadine-flavoured cream with the tart, though unflavoured whipped cream is also lovely here. Grenadine syrup is made from pomegranate juice, a flavour that also pairs really well with rhubarb and oranges.

Serves 6–8

1 To make the pastry, put the flour, chilled butter and a pinch of salt in a food processor. Pulse until the texture is similar to coarse breadcrumbs. Add the cream and **pulse again until the pastry barely comes together**. Remove to a floured work surface and gently bring the pastry together with your hands and form into a smooth, neat, flat disc. The pastry may appear a little streaky, but that is fine as it comes together beautifully in the cooking. Don't be tempted to knead the pastry, as you will toughen it. Wrap the pastry in cling film and chill in the fridge for 1 hour.

2 Preheat the oven to 200°C. Line a baking sheet with non-stick baking paper.

3 When ready to assemble the tart, flour your work surface and roll out the chilled pastry to a 36cm circle. If the edges of the pastry are a little uneven looking, that is fine, though the neater it is, the better the cooked tart will look. **Now place the pastry circle on the lined baking sheet.** Place the sliced rhubarb on the pastry to within **5cm of the edge**. Mix the sugar with the chopped vanilla pod and sprinkle **three-quarters** of it over the rhubarb. Fold in the rim of the pastry to hold the rhubarb in place and to leave an open face on the rhubarb where you now place the blood oranges in overlapping slices. Sprinkle on the remaining sugar.

4 Brush the surface of the pastry edge with a little beaten egg and sprinkle a little caster sugar over the egg.

5 Bake the tart in the oven for about 40 minutes, until the fruit is cooked and the pastry edge has a rich hazelnut colour. During the cooking some syrupy juice will escape from the tart, and **at intervals I spoon these juices back over the fruit to create a rich and delicious glaze**.

6 To make the grenadine cream, simply mix the cream and syrup together gently.

7 Remove the cooked tart from the oven and allow to cool a bit before serving. I like the tart best while still warm but not red hot from the oven. Serve the grenadine cream on the side.

Summer

MEAL 1

–

Salad of Oranges, Cucumber,
Marigold and Myrtle Berries
with Lemon Verbena Granita

–

Roast Wild Salmon with
Summer Leaves, Pea Tendrils,
Leaves and Flowers and
Preserved Lemon Dressing

–

Apricot Tart with Almond
Praline Cream

The pretty starter in this summer meal has two rather unusual ingredients that have only recently become part of my cooking. I have fallen in love with the scented marigold and the sweet myrtle berries that look and taste so good here. Neither are yet available to buy at your greengrocer, but I hope that will not frustrate you. As they become better known and as soon as restaurant chefs start to request them, the market will realise that there is a demand for them. But even without those two ingredients, this dish is still excellent. Both the marigold and myrtle are really easy to grow. The variety of myrtle is *Myrtus ugni* and the marigold is Golden Gem or Yellow Gem.

Wild salmon is a rare treat nowadays and it reminds us of the precarious position of our planet in relation to climate change. When I started cooking I could get as many of these magnificent wild fish as I could possibly want, but stocks have diminished at such an alarming rate in this part of the world that now I hardly ever see them. All the more reason to celebrate it, and this dish, with the piquant preserved lemon dressing and tender summer leaves, does just that. A bowl of boiled new potatoes (page 38) and perhaps some broad beans (page 60) or peas (page 73) would make this a perfect main course.

Apricots and almonds are one of those food matches made in heaven. I like to cook the tart until it is well coloured and crisp, by which time some of the apricots will have a little toasted line around their edges. This subtle line of colour adds a great depth of flavour to the tart, so be brave and follow suit.

Salad of Oranges, Cucumber, Marigold and Myrtle Berries with Lemon Verbena Granita

4 oranges, carefully segmented

2 tablespoons peeled, deseeded and very finely diced cucumber

2–4 teaspoons lemon juice

2 teaspoons honey

1 tablespoon tiny marigold leaves

1 tablespoon myrtle berries

4 dessertspoons lemon verbena granita (page 85)

2 teaspoons marigold leaves and flowers

The variety of marigold I like to use is Golden Gem or Yellow Gem. It is magical here, but not all marigold varieties have such an intriguing, scented flavour. If you can't find the marigold, you could happily replace it with lemon verbena. Myrtle berries, a beautiful sweet berry from Myrtus ugni, *are also not generally available, but as a garden plant to be grown in a pot or directly in the ground, it has few equals, both for the beauty of the berries beside the glossy green leaves and the delicious taste. These berries grow wild in County Kerry.*
Serves 4

1 Place the orange segments and diced cucumber in a bowl and add 2 teaspoons of the lemon juice and the honey. Stir very gently to mix, being careful not to break up the orange segments. Taste and if necessary correct the level of sweetness with a few more drops of lemon juice. Add the marigold leaves and myrtle berries to the bowl, mixing them in gently. Cover and chill until ready to serve.

2 To serve, divide the orange mixture and its juices between four shallow bowls. Place 1 dessertspoon of granita on top of the fruit and finally sprinkle on the marigold leaves and flowers. Serve immediately.

Lemon Verbena Granita

3 handfuls of lemon verbena leaves

225g caster sugar

600ml cold water

3 lemons

This recipe is simple, but watch out for the subtleties involved, such as using cold water with the sugar when cooking the leaves to draw out their flavour and allowing the syrup to cool completely before adding the lemon juice. The granita will keep for several weeks in the freezer but is considerably better when eaten as soon as possible after it has been frozen.

*This granita is good on its own but is even better when served with a splash of a dry sparkling wine. Serve as a light and refreshing dessert or even as a cooling starter on a scorching summer day. **Serves 6–8***

1   Place the leaves, sugar and **cold** water in a saucepan set over a moderate heat. Stir occasionally to encourage the sugar to dissolve and bring it to a simmer. Allow it to simmer gently for 2 minutes. Remove from the heat and allow to **cool completely**. You will end up with a pale green syrup.

2   Juice the lemons and add to the syrup, and right before your eyes you will see the green tinge disappear. Strain out the leaves through a sieve – I usually press on the leaves to extract as much flavour as I can. Place the strained syrup in a wide container and freeze until set.

3   Remove from the freezer and break up the ice with a fork. It will look like a slushy mess. Refreeze and repeat the process twice more – or three times if you can bear it – and eventually you will end up with the distinctive shard-like consistency of a granita. Refreeze, covered, until you are ready to serve. I serve it in coloured glasses or glass bowls with a single relevant leaf to decorate and a splash of chilled sparkling wine.

Roast Wild Salmon with Summer Leaves, Pea Tendrils, Leaves and Flowers and Preserved Lemon Dressing

4 x 150g darnes of wild salmon

1 tablespoon extra virgin olive oil

12–16 leaves of green oak leaf lettuce, washed and dried

12–16 pea tendrils, leaves and flowers (optional)

chervil or fennel sprigs, to garnish

flaky sea salt, to serve

Preserved lemon dressing

½ preserved lemon (page 261), seeds removed and flesh finely chopped

3 tablespoons extra virgin olive oil

1 tablespoon white wine vinegar

2 teaspoons honey

sea salt and freshly ground black pepper

*This is a simple dish to cook and serve and has a fresh, summery feel to it. The cooking time for roasting the salmon is short, as you want the fish to be just cooked through to the centre. The preserved lemon dressing is also great with grilled chicken or even a pork chop. The lettuce leaves wilt slightly on the hot plates and become more like a vegetable than a salad. The pea tendrils, leaves and flowers are optional, but when available are both pretty and delicious. The final addition to the plates of chervil or fennel sprigs adds a delicate aniseed flavour that I love. **Serves 4***

1 Preheat the oven to 220°C. Line a baking sheet with non-stick baking paper.
2 Mix all the dressing ingredients together, taste and correct the seasoning.
3 Rub the pieces of salmon all over with the olive oil and season with salt and pepper. Place on the lined sheet, skin side down, and cook in the oven for 10 minutes, **until just cooked through**.
4 Place the lettuce on hot plates and put a piece of cooked salmon on each one. Scatter on the pea leaves, flowers and tendrils (if using). Drizzle the dressing over the leaves and fish and garnish with sprigs of chervil or fennel. Add a few flakes of sea salt to each plate and serve immediately.

Apricot Tart with Almond Praline Cream

250g puff pastry (page 256)

450g fresh apricots, halved and
    stones removed

100g caster sugar

zest of 1 lemon

Almond praline cream

2 tablespoons almond praline
    powder (page 22)

4 tablespoons softly whipped cream

I love this classic combination of flavours. The quality of puff pastry you use for the tart base is crucial for a delicious buttery flavour and a non-greasy texture. I make my own and have included the recipe on page 256. The tart really needs the praline cream served with it, both for flavour and sweetness.
Serves 4–6

1 Preheat the oven to 200°C. Line a baking sheet with non-stick baking paper.

2 Roll the pastry out, cut into a neat 22cm circle and place on the lined baking sheet. To achieve a rim on the cooked tart, cut another circle **1cm in from the edge of the pastry**. Your knife should pierce the pastry about 1mm deep and should be an obvious cut, not just a mark. This 1cm rim will be the risen edge of the cooked tart and hold the fruit in place. Now pierce the pastry inside the 1cm rim all over with a fork, **making sure you feel the tines of the fork hitting the baking sheet**. Do not pierce outside the 1cm rim with your fork.

3 Mix the apricots, sugar and lemon zest together in a bowl. Arrange the apricots on the pastry in an upright, slightly slanted, slightly standing up and overlapping fashion, being careful to keep them **5mm inside the line on the pastry rim**. This will be a bit awkward, but a bit of manoeuvring will get them all into place. Fill the centre of the tart as well. It will look like too much fruit, but the tart really needs it all. Any sugar and lemon zest left in the bowl should be sprinkled over the apricots. Don't be tempted to leave out some of the sugar or the tart will be too bitter.

4 Bake the tart in the oven for 45 minutes. I like to **baste the tart with the syrupy cooking juices** after the tart has been cooking for 20 minutes and repeat the basting twice more at intervals. I like the tart to have plenty of colour and I love it when some of the apricots get a little black rim on the cut edge of the fruit.

5 Remove the cooked tart from the oven and allow to settle for 5 minutes before carefully transferring to a serving plate. Spoon any cooking juices from the baking sheet over the tart.

6 To make the almond praline cream, simply fold the praline powder into the whipped cream.

7 This tart is best served slightly warm with the chilled praline cream on the side.

MEAL 2

–

Potato Aioli with Quail Eggs,
Radishes, Cherry Tomatoes,
Spring Onions, Avocado,
Coriander and Cumin

–

Roasted Aubergine with
Ricotta, Honey, Mint, Fennel
and Chilli

–

Chocolate Soufflé Cake with
Chocolate Sauce

The starter in this meal makes a colourful and amusing presentation, with the radishes and cherry tomatoes sitting up straight amongst the other ingredients. On another day, tiny carrots, equally petite courgettes, pea pods and crisp watercress sprigs would also have a place sitting on top of the potato aioli. This is a fun dish but nonetheless delicious and may be a way of introducing hesitant younger eaters to the joys of vegetables. The overall effect of the presentation should be that of a mini garden full of super-fresh vegetables.

Aubergines are an absolute favourite vegetable of mine. I think it's amazing how they will happily sit with the flavours of most of the world's major food cultures. Here they are roasted until tender and lightly glazed with honey, olive oil, fennel seeds and chilli. This part of the process can be done early on in the day. Finishing the dish will then be easy, with just a dollop of fresh ricotta and a piquant dressing to pull all the flavours together. In this menu this dish is the main course, but it would make a good starter in another meal. I don't see why both the starter and the main course in this meal could not come to the table at the same time for a lovely combined meat-free experience.

The chocolate soufflé cake is rather decadent, though it does not present itself with all bells and whistles blaring. Relatively simple in appearance, it is not until you taste it that the beauty of the cake really comes through. The texture is both light and luscious at the same time. Softly whipped cream, raspberries and a spoonful or two of chocolate sauce will have chocolate lovers swooning. At another time of year, the jasmine tea-soaked prunes on page 52 would be a good replacement for the raspberries.

Potato Aioli with Quail Eggs, Radishes, Cherry Tomatoes, Spring Onions, Avocado, Coriander and Cumin

3 medium potatoes (about 375g)

1 garlic clove, peeled and crushed to a paste

2 tablespoons homemade mayonnaise (page 258)

1 tablespoon chopped fresh parsley

1 tablespoon chopped fresh chives

sea salt and freshly ground black pepper

Dressing

3 tablespoons extra virgin olive oil

1 tablespoon lemon juice

To serve

12 quail eggs or 3 hen's eggs

18 radishes

18 cherry tomatoes

6 small spring onions

2 avocados, halved, stoned, peeled and each cut into 9 wedges (optional)

18 fresh coriander leaves

1 teaspoon roasted and ground cumin seeds

This is a pretty and fun dish that you can serve without cutlery, as the vegetable and quail egg garnishes can be drawn through the potato aioli with your fingers and popped into the mouth. Or you can of course make life simple and lay the table with cutlery.

The dish can be assembled on individual plates or on one large flat serving dish, though in the case of the latter you need to be sure that it is being served to guests who are happy to share, which is not everyone's cup of tea. Think of this dish as a vehicle for the very best and freshest vegetables of the season and expand on the ingredient list accordingly. Baby carrots, pea pods and tiny courgettes are some of the other seasonal treats that I occasionally add to this dish. **Serves 6**

1 Cook the potatoes in boiling salted water until tender, which should take about 30 minutes. Depending on the variety of potato being used it may be necessary, as in the case of a floury Golden Wonder or Kerr's Pink, to strain off some of the cooking water during the cooking and to finish cooking the potatoes in just a few centimetres of water. When the potatoes are cooked, strain and **save at least 5 tablespoons of the cooking water**.

2 Peel the cooked potatoes immediately and pass through a vegetable mouli or a potato ricer to achieve a soft mash. Add the reserved cooking water along with the garlic, mayonnaise , parsley and chives and mix well. Taste and correct the seasoning. This part of the recipe can be made early on.

3 Carefully lower the quail eggs into a saucepan of boiling salted water and cook for 6 minutes. Drain and allow to cool, then peel and cut each one in half.

4 To make the dressing, mix the oil, lemon juice and seasoning together. Taste and correct the seasoning.

5   To assemble the dish, spread 1 tablespoon of the potato aioli in a circle on each plate. Divide the halved quail eggs, radishes, tomatoes, spring onions and avocado pieces between the plates, all sitting up proud as punch, and scatter on some coriander leaves. (If I have a few tiny carrots or courgettes, I will also add those and omit the avocado.) Finish each plate with a drizzle of the well-mixed dressing and a good pinch of the ground cumin.

Roasted Aubergine with Ricotta, Honey, Mint, Fennel and Chilli

1 aubergine (about 300g), cut crossways into 12 round slices

Roasting oil

4 tablespoons extra virgin olive oil

1 teaspoon roasted and coarsely ground fennel seeds

1 teaspoon honey

pinch of chilli flakes

sea salt and freshly ground black pepper

Dressing

3 tablespoons extra virgin olive oil

1 tablespoon finely chopped fresh mint leaves

1 tablespoon finely chopped anchovy

1 tablespoon lemon juice

1 teaspoon roasted and coarsely ground fennel seeds

½ teaspoon honey

pinch of chilli flakes

To finish

200g ricotta

20 fresh mint leaves

This makes a light, delicious starter or a lunch or supper dish, as being served here. All the elements of this dish can be prepared in advance and assembled later. **Serves 4**

1 Preheat the oven to 200°C. Line a baking tray with non-stick baking paper.

2 Mix all the ingredients for the roasting oil in a bowl until well combined. The honey may fall to the bottom of the mixture, so stir it well. Paint both sides of the aubergine slices with the dressing and place on the lined tray. The oil may seem a bit scant, but it will be enough. Roast in the oven for about 30 minutes, until slightly coloured and tender to touch. I usually **turn them halfway through the cooking time** to ensure a good even colour.

3 Mix all the dressing ingredients together and correct the seasoning.

4 To assemble, divide the aubergine slices between four plates, allowing three per serving, or assemble on one large serving dish to be served family style. Divide the ricotta between the aubergines and spoon over the dressing. Sprinkle with the fresh mint leaves and serve.

Chocolate Soufflé Cake with Chocolate Sauce

melted butter, for greasing

200g chocolate (at least 55% cocoa solids), coarsely chopped

6 eggs

150g caster sugar

110ml milk

1 teaspoon vanilla extract

To serve

a dusting of bitter cocoa powder

fresh raspberries

softly whipped cream

chocolate sauce (page 98)

This is one of those cakes that rises up beautifully as it bakes, then proceeds to collapse when it comes out of the oven. That's okay though, as the resulting soft, mousse-like texture is wonderful. Serving chocolate sauce with the cake may seem excessive, but believe me, it is really spectacular. Other than that, a bowl of fresh raspberries and softly whipped cream are all that you need. **Serves 8–10**

1 Preheat the oven to 180°C. Grease a 20cm springform tin with melted butter and place a disc of non-stick baking paper on the base.

2 Put the chocolate in a Pyrex bowl and sit it over a saucepan of cold water, making sure that the bottom of the bowl is not touching the water in the saucepan. Bring the water to a simmer, then turn off the heat to allow the chocolate to melt slowly.

3 Separate the eggs and place the whites in a spotlessly clean bowl.

4 When the chocolate has melted, whisk in the egg yolks, **half of the sugar**, the milk and vanilla extract.

5 Whisk the egg whites while gradually adding the remaining sugar. You want to achieve a set snow with a glossy, meringue-like consistency.

6 Stir one-quarter of the beaten egg white into the chocolate mixture and fold the rest in gently but thoroughly. Scrape the batter into the prepared springform tin and gently smooth the top.

7 Bake the cake in the oven for 30 minutes. After 20 minutes it may be necessary to place a sheet of non-stick baking paper over the top of the cake if it is colouring too quickly. By now the cake will look like a risen soufflé. Continue cooking for a further 10 minutes.

8 Remove from the oven and place on a wire rack to allow the cake to cool completely before removing from the tin. The cake will deflate slightly to create a wonderful foamy consistency. Dust the cake with the cocoa powder just before serving and serve with a few fresh raspberries, softly whipped cream and chocolate sauce if you are really going for it!

Chocolate Sauce

150g best-quality chocolate (at least
    62% cocoa solids), finely chopped

75ml cream

75ml milk

½ teaspoon vanilla extract or
    1 tablespoon rum

I have several different recipes for chocolate sauce, but I think this rather uncomplicated one is best with the chocolate soufflé cake on page 96. **Serves 8–10**

Place the chocolate, cream, milk and vanilla in a small saucepan and melt over a low heat, whisking occasionally, until the sauce is smooth and a rich, glossy colour. Keep the chocolate sauce in a warm place, such as sitting in the saucepan that you melted it in with the heat turned off.

This meal is full of sparkling summer flavours. To start with, Irish mozzarella from County Cork is paired with courgette, lemon and marjoram. That is not necessarily surprising, except that the lemon is candied and the resulting slightly chewy, sticky citrus texture and flavour are unexpected but quite wonderful.

The courgettes should be small for this dish, as they are being served raw. In food cultures where the courgette is better known and understood than in ours, there are different recipes and cooking techniques for courgettes at the various different stages of growth, from the small ones we are using here served raw to large oversized ones, which will often be slowly stewed to achieve an entirely different result.

I remember as a school boy singing the line 'the corn is as high as an elephant's eye' from the musical *Oklahoma!*, the meaning of which I did not really understand until I actually saw corn plants growing tall and looking as if they were 'climbin' clear up to the sky'. The flavoursome and sweet-tasting corn purée with chilli and lime can be prepared in advance and reheated later to serve with the roast beef. The piquant red onions can also be prepared ahead of time, thus minimising the last-minute effort here. This combination is equally good with grilled beef as it is with roast beef.

I love the balsamic-glazed potatoes as the accompanying vegetable and would often serve a green vegetable such as French or runner beans as well (page 262). Look out for the rather flat-looking Romano bean – it is one of the best I have tasted.

There is a bit of commitment required for the dessert here, though the jelly and granita element can be made in advance. I think this combination of flavours and textures is a bull's eye. Strawberries and elderflower are fabulous together and the icy flakes of granita with the lightly jellied strawberries, crushed berries and softly whipped cream is rather dreamy.

All in all, this should be a great meal to eat.

Macroom Buffalo Mozzarella with Courgettes, Candied Lemon and Marjoram

1 unwaxed lemon

35g caster sugar

2 small courgettes, about 15cm long

4 tablespoons extra virgin olive oil

2 tablespoons lemon juice

sea salt and freshly ground
   black pepper

2 x 125g balls of Macroom buffalo
   mozzarella

1 tablespoon sweet marjoram leaves

This is an unexpected combination of flavours that works beautifully. It is very exciting to be able to source mozzarella that has been produced in Ireland from the milk of buffalo that are grazing on Irish grass. Finding that mozzarella from Macroom in County Cork is a priority for me when making this dish. Use small courgettes here so that they taste nutty and have a crisp texture. A combination of green and golden courgettes makes a particularly pretty presentation. If the flowers are still attached to them, just tear them into little strips and add them to the salad. Serves 4

1 Using a swivel-top peeler, peel the lemon rind into thin strips and cut the strips lengthways into a fine julienne. Place in a small saucepan of **cold water** and bring to a simmer, then strain and cool under cold running water. Put back in the saucepan with the caster sugar. Squeeze the peeled lemon and add enough water to the lemon juice so that you have 100ml of liquid. Pour into the saucepan and **simmer very gently** for 10–15 minutes, until the lemon appears candied and translucent and the syrup has thickened slightly. Allow to cool.

2 To assemble the salad, cut the courgettes lengthways into very thin slices about 3mm thick (not paper thin) and place in a small bowl. Dress immediately with the olive oil and lemon juice, season with salt and pepper and taste to correct the seasoning.

3 Divide the courgettes between four plates in a flat layer. Spread them out a bit, as you will want to see their lovely colour under the mozzarella. Tear each ball of mozzarella in half and place on the courgettes. Place a pinch of candied peel on top of the mozzarella and a few strands around the courgettes. Drizzle a little syrup on top and any liquid remaining from dressing the courgettes. Sprinkle the marjoram leaves over everything, add a final pinch of sea salt and serve immediately.

Roast Sirloin of Beef with Creamed Corn and Pickled Red Onions

2.5kg sirloin of beef on the bone

sea salt and freshly ground
   black pepper

To serve

creamed corn (page 104)

pickled red onions (page 105)

rustic roast potatoes with balsamic
   butter (page 107)

The combination of the creamy corn purée spiked with hot chilli and cooling lime acts as a good foil for the rich beef. The pickled onions, which can be prepared hours or days ahead, lighten and enliven the whole dish.

The sirloin of beef on the bone is a fantastic cut and somewhat easier to carve than the more traditional wing rib. This is another of those cuts of meat that will be best if ordered from your butcher a bit in advance so as to give your butcher time to put aside a piece of properly hung beef for you. Like most cuts of meat, especially the larger ones, the roast will sit quite happily for at least half an hour after cooking. I often use a grilled steak or hamburger in place of the roast beef in this recipe. **Serves 6–8**

1 Begin by preparing the corn purée and pickled onions on the following pages.
2 Preheat the oven to 240°C.
3 Lightly score the fat on the surface of the beef, then place on a roasting tin and season the beef with salt and pepper. Roast in the oven for 15 minutes before reducing the temperature to 180°C and cooking the beef to your liking. A roast of this size will need to cook for a further 35 minutes for rare, 45 minutes for medium and 75 minutes for well done.
4 When the beef is cooked, remove it from the oven and reduce the temperature again to 100°C. Allow to rest and keep warm in the low oven for at least 15 minutes and up to 1 hour before carving.
5 To serve, reheat the corn purée to a bubble and spread it out over hot plates. Place one or two slices of beef on top and scatter over a few pickled onions. Finish with a drizzle of any beef cooking juices and a sprinkle of sea salt and serve immediately with the rustic roast potatoes on the side.

Creamed Corn

4 cooked ears of corn

50g butter

juice of 1 lime

1 medium-hot chilli, deseeded and
    coarsely chopped

sea salt and freshly ground
    black pepper

175ml sour cream

120ml chicken stock (page 257)

I prefer to use fresh summer corn in this dish but I have also made it with cooked frozen corn and the result was excellent, so this dish can be a year-round possibility. The corn can be prepared early in the day or even the previous day if you wish. It will thicken a little when prepared in advance, but I add some chicken stock, vegetable stock or water to it when reheating and it works perfectly. **Serves 6–8**

1   Preheat the grill to high or your oven to 250°C or as hot as it will go.
2   Cut the kernels off the cooked ears of corn and place on a roasting tray. Add the butter, lime juice (I put the squeezed rinds on the tray too) and the chopped chilli and season with salt and pepper. Mix everything together and spread out to cover the tray.
3   Place under a hot grill or in your hottest oven and cook for about 15 minutes, until the corn is getting charred. I stir the contents of the tray a couple of times during the cooking time to ensure the corn colours evenly.
4   When the corn is sufficiently coloured, **remove the lime rinds** and squeeze the soft pulp back onto the corn. Scrape the contents of the tray into a blender with the sour cream and chicken stock. Blend to a slightly coarse purée, then taste and correct the seasoning. The corn reheats perfectly, but you may need to add a little more chicken stock or water to loosen the mixture.

Pickled Red Onions

2 red onions, peeled and very
  thinly sliced
2 tablespoons cider, red wine or
  white wine vinegar
1 tablespoon caster sugar
pinch of salt

These piquant onions could not be much simpler. Apart from serving them with the beef and corn purée in this meal, I also serve them with a beef or lamb burger, with a sharp Cheddar cheese, with smoked or marinated fish and with most cold roast meats. **Makes 1 jar**

Mix all the ingredients together in a non-reactive bowl and allow the onions to wilt, which will take about 30 minutes. The onions will keep covered in the fridge for weeks.

Rustic Roast Potatoes with Balsamic Butter

900g potatoes (preferably
   Golden Wonder)

2 garlic cloves, skin on and
   lightly bashed

2 large sprigs of fresh rosemary

4 tablespoons extra virgin olive oil,
   duck or goose fat

50g butter

4 tablespoons balsamic vinegar

sea salt and freshly ground
   black pepper

When in Ireland I eat only Irish potatoes, preferably from Ballycotton in County Cork where I live, and I always buy them unscrubbed, or in other words, with some of the earth they grew in still attached. Pre-scrubbed potatoes lose a lot of their flavour and texture between being scrubbed and getting to your kitchen. The difference is quite extraordinary and it seems such a pity to lose the magical quality of the Irish potato for the sake of a few minutes of scrubbing. My favourite variety of potato for this dish is the Golden Wonder.

The combination of potato, butter, balsamic vinegar, rosemary and a hint of garlic is hard to beat. These potatoes are also great with lamb or venison or to serve with any dish where a crispy, flavoursome potato is required. **Serves 6**

1 Preheat the oven to 220°C.

2 Scrub the potatoes until spotlessly clean. There is no need to peel them. Cut the potatoes in half lengthways and then into wedges rather than chips. Put in a bowl with the garlic and rosemary and drizzle on the olive oil or fat. Turn the potatoes in the fat to coat lightly. There should not be a pool of fat in the bottom of the bowl, but the potatoes should be covered with a thin sheen of fat. Do not season the potatoes until they are cooked, as it tends to cause the potatoes to stick to the roasting tray and you may lose the crispy skins.

3 Place the potatoes on a roasting tray in a single layer, skin side down and ideally with a little space between each potato, and scatter the garlic and rosemary between the wedges. Roast in the oven for about 35 minutes, until the skins are crispy and the centres are tender. **Avoid the temptation to move them on the tray halfway through the cooking time**, as this will only break up the potato skins. The potatoes will eventually crisp up and

loosen from the bottom of the tray.

4 When cooked, remove from the oven and immediately add the butter and vinegar to the tray with a seasoning of salt and pepper. Toss the potatoes to glaze them in the melting butter and vinegar and serve immediately.

Strawberry and Elderflower Jelly with Elderflower Granita, Crushed Strawberries and Cream

2 large handfuls of
   elderflower heads
225g caster or granulated sugar
600ml cold water
juice of 3 lemons
300ml crushed fresh strawberries
   (I use an old-fashioned potato
   masher for this)
2 teaspoons powdered gelatine
2 tablespoons cold water
grapeseed or sunflower oil,
   for greasing
200g fresh strawberries, for
   final assembly
2–4 tablespoons elderflower cordial
6 tablespoons softly whipped cream
2 fresh elderflower heads,
   if available

Wobbly jelly, chilly ice, crushed berries and softly whipped cream all add up to strawberries and cream with a new dimension. There is bit of preparation to be done with the granita and the jelly, but all of that can happen a day or two ahead. The final assembly is quite quick and I promise that this will make your family and friends hum with pleasure.
Serves 6

1 For the granita and the jelly, place the elderflowers, sugar and 600ml of cold water in a stainless steel saucepan. Bring to a simmer while occasionally stirring to encourage the sugar to dissolve. Simmer very gently for 1 minute, then remove from the heat and allow to cool completely. Add the lemon juice and mix well, then strain through a fine sieve, pressing hard to extract as much of the liquid as possible. **Reserve 300ml of this liquid for the jelly.**

2 Place the remaining liquid in a wide container and freeze until it is beginning to set at the edges. Break up the mixture with a fork to a sludgy consistency and refreeze. **Repeat this process of freezing and breaking up the mixture another three times** to achieve a coarse granita texture.

3 To make the jelly, add the 300ml of crushed strawberries to the reserved elderflower liquid to attain **exactly 600ml** of the mixture.

4 Put the gelatine in a Pyrex jug or bowl, then pour over the 2 tablespoons of cold water and allow to set and become sponge-like in appearance. Set the jug or bowl in a saucepan of water and bring to the gentlest simmer to allow the gelatine to dissolve to a clear liquid, then remove from the heat. **Add 6 tablespoons of the strawberry and elderflower mixture to the dissolved gelatine and mix well, then add this back into the remaining strawberry and elderflower mixture and stir well.**

5 Lightly oil 6 x 100ml dariole moulds or one large serving dish with a tasteless oil such as grapeseed or sunflower oil. Divide the mixture between the oiled moulds or the dish and allow to set in the fridge for a minimum of 2 hours.

6 To serve, chill six deep plates. Crush the remaining 200g of strawberries and add the elderflower cordial to taste. Divide the crushed berries between the plates. Unmold the jellies and nestle them into the strawberries. If you have used a large container to set the jelly in, just spoon or cut out the jelly to the size and shape you require.

7 Place a scoop of granita on top of each jelly and top with 1 tablespoon of the softly whipped cream. If fresh elderflowers are available, I sprinkle on some of the tiny flowers at this point. Serve immediately.

All the flavours in the salad to start this meal are entirely happy together and it makes for a very satisfying dish. The homemade mayonnaise and harissa are what elevate a simple enough combination to something really good. If you try this with the well-known brand of mayonnaise and a generic tin of harissa, you may not be happy with the result. With a pot of boiled new potatoes (page 38), it would make a perfect meal on its own.

I find the squid delightful both in taste and appearance. If you are nervous about preparing it, ask your fishmonger to do it for you and keep a close eye on the process, then next time you can thrill all at home with the magic that unfolds as you prepare the fish yourself. Ask to bring home the feather-shaped transparent quill removed from the fish and make sure to show it to everyone around the table to marvel at the mystery and magnificence of nature. Once your tomatoes are ready, cooking the fish and assembling the dish is quick and easy.

I think the spaghetti and courgettes are the perfect accompaniment to the squid – the textures and flavours are all great together – but grilled bread doused with olive oil (page 16) would be good instead of the spaghetti and would be perfect for mopping up the tomato juices.

Where has fruit salad disappeared to? It used to be a staple on many restaurant menus, but perhaps that is the reason for its flight into hiding, as it ceased to be taken seriously by cooks and as a result was just not delicious to eat. However, with the correct choice of seasonal fruit, it is a light, smart, glistening conclusion to a meal. You could serve a little cream with it here. The elderflower granita on page 109 or jasmine tea parfait on page 51 would also be great with it.

Salad of Hard-boiled Eggs with Chorizo, Mayonnaise and Harissa

50g cured chorizo, casing removed
  and thinly sliced

4 tablespoons extra virgin olive oil

4 eggs

4 large handfuls of rocket leaves or
  mixed salad leaves

2–4 teaspoons harissa (page 264)

1–2 tablespoons homemade
  mayonnaise (page 258)

a few drops of red wine or
  sherry vinegar

This is an utterly simple salad to make, but be sure to get the best chorizo and eggs and the salad will be as delicious as it is easy. This would make a perfect lunch or supper dish if accompanied by the rustic roast potatoes with balsamic butter on page 107.

*If you don't use all the chorizo-flavoured oil on the salad, keep it covered in the fridge and use it for frying cooked potatoes or roasting vegetables at a later time. The chilled oil will keep perfectly for several weeks. **Serves 4***

1 Heat the chorizo very gently in the olive oil by **bringing it barely to a simmer, then immediately removing from the heat**. Don't allow the oil to boil, as this will toughen the chorizo. The chorizo can rest in the oil for 30 minutes.

1 Hard-boil the eggs by lowering them gently into a saucepan of **boiling salted water** and cooking them at a boil for exactly 10 minutes. If you don't want the yolk to be completely hard, cook for 9 minutes. The salt in the water seasons the egg and will help to coagulate any white that might seep out of a crack in the shell, hence less leakage. Remove from the saucepan immediately with a slotted spoon and cool under a cold running tap. Peel each egg and cut in half lengthways.

2 To assemble, scatter the leaves onto a large serving platter. Place the hard-boiled eggs among the leaves, then place the chorizo slices on the leaves in between the eggs. Drizzle a little harissa onto the eggs, then do the same with the mayonnaise. Finally, drizzle on some of the chorizo-flavoured oil and a few drops of red wine or sherry vinegar and serve immediately.

Grilled Squid with Roasted Cherry Tomatoes and Marjoram

4 squid, weighing about 250g each
    after being cleaned

20 ripe, firm cherry tomatoes

sea salt and freshly ground
    black pepper

1 garlic clove, peeled and
    finely sliced

1 branch of fresh thyme

1 tablespoon balsamic vinegar

1 tablespoon extra virgin olive oil,
    plus extra for drizzling

1 tablespoon fresh marjoram or
    thyme leaves

zest of 1 lemon

Squid requires either very quick or very slow cooking. I cook it for a few minutes on a hot pan, as in this recipe, or slowly stew it for about an hour. Anything in between and you will end up with a rather chewy dish. Preparing the fish is without doubt one of my favourite kitchen tasks and I never cease to be amazed when I remove the long slender quill with its feather-like shape and intriguingly clear plastic appearance and feel. The black ink explains why squid is sometimes called 'the scribe of the sea'. The tentacles also have their charm and the sac, when opened out, as in this recipe, looks like a rather sinister cloak. All in all, the preparation of the fish is one of the most visually pleasing and satisfying jobs. Avoid fish that are too big, as they will be tough and unpleasant if quickly cooked like I suggest here.

I am serving the squid as a main course in this meal, but it could also be served as a starter. **Serves 4**

1 Preheat a grill to maximum or an oven to 220°C.

2 Begin by preparing the squid. Cut off the tentacles in one piece in front of the eyes and remove the hard beak. Discard all the entrails. Catch the tip of the quill and pull it out of the sac. Pull the wings off the sac and wash both the wings and the sac, removing any grey or purple membrane. Cut the sac open by cutting along the line where the quill was removed. Wash away any remaining entrails. The sac will now look like a small cloak on your worktop. Score the sac all over by cutting about 1mm into the flesh in a criss-cross pattern on both sides of the flesh. Then cut the scored sac into four or six 8cm squares. This is approximate, so don't worry about being exact here. Lightly score the wings on both sides to prevent them from curling up the second they land on the hot pan. Chill until needed.

3 Place the cherry tomatoes in a small ovenproof frying pan or low-sided saucepan that they will fit into snugly. Season with salt and pepper and add the garlic, thyme and balsamic vinegar. Place under the grill or in the oven and cook for 15–20 minutes, turning occasionally, until the tomatoes are completely soft and somewhat blistered.

4 Remove the pan from the grill or oven, place on a medium heat on the hob and reduce until the cooking juices have become a syrupy glaze. **This will only take a matter of moments, so make sure not to render the tomatoes to a purée.**

5 Heat a heavy-bottomed grill pan or frying pan on a high heat. Dry the squid with kitchen paper and toss it in the olive oil. Season with salt and pepper and place on the very hot pan. Don't touch it for at least 2 minutes, until well coloured. Turn when you are happy with the colour and cook for 1 minute on the other side.

6 Divide between four hot plates and spoon the tomatoes and their juices around and over the fish. Sprinkle each serving with some marjoram or thyme leaves and lemon zest, a pinch of sea salt and a final drizzle of olive oil.

Peach Popsicles, *p133*

Chilled Tomato Water
with Lemon Basil, *p126*

Roast Sirloin of Beef with Creamed
Corn and Pickled Red Onions, *p102*

Spaghetti with Courgettes and Marjoram

600g courgettes (450g after
    removing the watery seeds)
sea salt and freshly ground
    black pepper
300g spaghetti
4 tablespoons extra virgin olive oil
3 garlic cloves, peeled and
    thinly sliced
pinch of chilli flakes
zest of 1 lemon and some juice
    to taste
2 tablespoons chopped fresh
    marjoram leaves

This is a great combination of flavours and textures. You could add a few pieces of cooked pulled pork or ham to transform it into a lunch or supper dish. Cook and shelled mussels, shrimp or a dice of smoked salmon added to the finished dish would also produce a lovely family meal. **Serves 6–8**

1 Cut the courgettes from top to tail, first in half and then in quarters. Cut out any watery seeds and discard. Cut the flesh into long, thin strips about the same width as the spaghetti. Place in a colander, sprinkle with a little salt and mix through. Allow to rest over a bowl for 15 minutes, by which time they will be glistening with the moisture that the salt has drawn out of the flesh. Rinse briefly with cold water and dry thoroughly.

2 Bring 4 litres of water to a boil and add 2 teaspoons of salt. Add the spaghetti and allow to wilt into the water, giving it an occasional gentle stir. Cook according to the packet instructions, until the spaghetti is just al dente. Strain and **reserve about 100ml of the cooking water** for loosening the cooked pasta later. Return the strained pasta to the cooking pan and cover with a lid.

3 To finish the dish, heat a large frying pan or wok over a high heat. Add the olive oil and when hot add the garlic and allow to become golden, stirring throughout the brief time that it takes to colour it. Immediately add the chilli flakes and stir for a few seconds before adding the dried courgettes and seasoning with salt and pepper. Continue cooking and stirring on a high heat until the courgettes are cooked, which should take about 5 minutes. They will have picked up a little colour and be shiny.

4 Add the spaghetti to the courgette pan and stir well to mix. I use a kitchen tongs here, as the courgettes tend to fall to the bottom of the pan. If the spaghetti has clung together while resting, as it sometimes does, just sprinkle it with a little of the reserved pasta cooking water and allow the water to drain off. A quick stir now will loosen the spaghetti back into individual strands.

5 Add the grated lemon zest and a good squeeze of lemon juice to taste and correct the seasoning. Finish with a sprinkling of marjoram and serve immediately.

Summer Salad of Peaches, Strawberries, Raspberries and Blueberries

4–6 ripe peaches or nectarines

2 tablespoons caster sugar

juice of 1 lemon

150g fresh strawberries

150g fresh raspberries

150g fresh blueberries

Fruit salad, once a staple on many restaurant menus, has completely gone out of fashion. You are most likely to see it nowadays in a plastic container sitting in a chill counter as a breakfast offering. Perhaps some feel it is not smart enough to serve as a sweet after dinner, which is a pity, as it can be a refreshing and colourful end to a meal, whether served on its own or accompanied by an ice or a simple bowl of softly whipped cream. A thin biscuit, such as langues de chat (page 168), served alongside will smarten up the whole experience. Clearly, choosing fruit that is perfectly ripe and in season is the guaranteed way to a sparkling result. I prefer not to add any flavouring to the fruit with the exception of either some tiny fresh mint or lemon basil leaves, but the lemon verbena granita on page 85 or jasmine tea parfait page 51 would make a delicious and stylish accompaniment. **Serves 4**

1 To peel the peaches, cut a small shallow cross in the stem end of the fruit. Place in a heatproof bowl and pour over boiling water to cover the fruit – the water must be absolutely boiling. Count out **10 seconds** and immediately remove the fruit with a slotted spoon and gently submerge them in a bowl of iced water. After a few seconds, remove them from the chilled water and the skins should slip off easily. Cut the peaches off the stone into slices 5mm thick and place in a bowl. Sprinkle them with a little sugar and a few drops of lemon juice as you go. Depending on how sweet the fruit is, you may not need all the sugar and be mean with the lemon juice, as you don't want its flavour and sharpness to dominate. The lemon juice is in this dish to prevent the peaches from discolouring and to enhance the flavour of the fruit with its acidity.

2 When all the peaches have been sliced, cut the strawberries into quarters and add to the peaches along with the raspberries and blueberries. **Mix gently with a flexible rubber spatula.** The sugar will already be dissolving to a delicious syrup. Taste, being sure to get a piece of each fruit on the spoon, and decide if you need to add any of the remaining sugar.

3 Serve the fruit salad as soon as the sugar has all dissolved to a rich syrup, or cover and chill for serving later.

This is a meal that will hopefully be enjoyed on a warm sunny evening in the garden. There is a slightly whimsical nature to the tomato water and the popsicles that is fun, but more importantly, they are really delicious. Both the water and popsicles can be prepared in advance, as can all the elements for the main course of little lamb koftas.

The tomato water is a surprising and marvellously light beginning to a summer meal. The ripest tomatoes are required and the clear liquid you end up with gives nothing away as to the flavour burst that ensues. If I am serving the meal al fresco I use glasses, as they make drinking the tomato water rather easier. The glasses lined up on a tray with a cherry tomato and lemon basil garnish look pretty and festive. If you get a little evening sunshine slanting through the glasses, all the better.

The goats' cheese and fig salad is an extra course in this meal, but given the lightness of the tomato water to start with, the overall effect of this meal should be summery and refreshing. Serving two salad-type dishes in the same meal may also appear unbalanced, but I think that only adds to the suitability of the dishes as a lovely summer meal.

Hot and juicy lamb koftas sitting on a bed of leaves with a tangy yet cooling creamy dressing, a sprinkle of cumin, crunchy roasted hazelnuts and a drizzle of hot chilli oil both looks beautiful and tastes great. I suggest purslane in the salad recipe, but failing that, rocket leaves make an excellent substitute. The dressing of yogurt, buttermilk and garlic is a perfect foil for the chilli oil that is drizzled over the salad.

The popsicles look terrific and their depth of flavour will surprise. They are simple to serve and the langues de chat biscuit that I suggest to serve with them will bring a smile to all faces.

Chilled Tomato Water with Lemon Basil

1kg very ripe tomatoes

14 fresh lemon or sweet basil leaves

1 teaspoon caster sugar

1 teaspoon Maldon sea salt

pinch of cracked black pepper

To serve

8 tiny cherry tomatoes, peeled

4 tiny fresh lemon or sweet
basil leaves

4 teaspoons best-quality extra
virgin olive oil, such as Fontodi
or Capezzana

You will need the ripest tomatoes for this exquisite essence of tomatoes. If you can't find the wonderful lemon basil, the more easily available sweet basil works well too. Use the finest olive oil to drizzle on the water just before serving. I use the tiniest little cherry tomatoes I can find for serving in the water.
Serves 4

1 Cut the tomatoes into coarse pieces and place in a large bowl. Tear up the basil leaves and add to the bowl with the sugar, salt and pepper. Use a hand-held blender to pulse the ingredients to a **rough, coarse purée, but don't over-blend**, as you will end up with a cloudy water that will spoil the appearance of the dish.

2 Place the mixture in a large square of clean muslin, tie securely and hang over a bowl to allow the water to drip into it. I allow the tomatoes to drip for a minimum of 4 hours and sometimes overnight. Chill the drained tomato water. The purée remaining in the square of muslin can be added to a vegetable stock.

3 When ready to serve, taste the tomato water and adjust accordingly with salt and pepper to ensure a perfect seasoning. Serve in small bowls or glasses, adding two of the peeled cherry tomatoes to each serving along with a basil leaf. Finally, drizzle 1 teaspoon of olive oil on each serving and serve immediately.

Salad of Fresh Figs, Goats' Cheese and Mint

16–20 rocket leaves

4 ripe figs

4 slices of soft goats' cheese, such
as Ardsallagh or St Tola

16–20 small fresh mint leaves

Dressing

3 tablespoons extra virgin olive oil

1 tablespoon lemon juice

1 teaspoon honey

sea salt and freshly ground
black pepper

This is a simple and effective little salad that can be served as a first course or as a cheese course. In a recipe such as this with a short ingredients list and no cooking, but rather just assembling the ingredients involved, the quality of your ingredients is paramount. Make sure your figs are beautifully ripe and tender and that the goats' cheese is soft and sweetly fresh.

If I am serving this dish at the end of a meal I sometimes add a few fresh raspberries, which pair beautifully with the other ingredients, and then I have cheese and a sweet in a single course. A few pomegranate seeds are also a good addition. **Serves 4**

1 Divide the rocket leaves between four plates or one large serving dish. Cut the figs in half and then into quarters down through the stalk, all the time keeping it hinged at the base so as to maintain a good shape. If the figs fall apart, don't worry at all, but just change your presentation and place the fig quarters randomly around the plate. Place the cut figs in the centre of the plates or on the leaves on the large serving dish.

2 Slice the goats' cheese and place a slice in the centre of each fig 'flower'.

3 Mix all the dressing ingredients well and season to taste with salt and pepper.

4 Drizzle the dressing over the figs, goats' cheese and leaves, then scatter the mint leaves over the plates and serve.

Lamb Koftas

450g minced lamb shoulder

100g raw onion, peeled and grated on a box grater to a paste

1 medium-hot fresh red chilli, deseeded and finely chopped

1 garlic clove, peeled and grated on a Microplane grater to a paste

2 tablespoons chopped fresh or dried hyssop or 2 pinches of za'atar

1 dessertspoon date syrup

sea salt and freshly ground black pepper

extra virgin olive oil, for frying

grated zest of 1 lemon

To serve

salad of purslane with buttermilk dressing, chilli oil, roasted hazelnuts and cumin (page 131)

boiled new potatoes (page 38)

This recipe came about when friends sent me a holiday photograph from Turkey of a delicious lunch they were enjoying. I set about recreating what I believed the image to be and am very happy with the result. When served with the salad of purslane or rocket leaves with buttermilk dressing on page 131, the koftas really are a joy.

Sweet minced lamb is the basis for the recipe and it is really important that the lamb is freshly minced and that it has a good proportion of fat (about 10%) to ensure you get tender, juicy koftas. I usually specify shoulder of lamb to my butcher.

I grow hyssop in my garden and dry some every year, though the exotic-sounding za'atar, a Middle Eastern blend of dried herbs and spices, is now easily available and adds a deeply authentic flavour to the dish. Date syrup, another relatively recent arrival to my larder, adds a sweetness and shiny lustre to the koftas.

I like to roll these into little balls the size of a large grape, but they can of course be made bigger into burger or sausage shapes.

Makes 50 small koftas

1 Mix together all the ingredients for the koftas except the olive oil and lemon zest. Fry a tiny piece in a frying pan to check the flavour and adjust the seasoning accordingly. Form into little balls approximately 10g each and store on a baking tray lined with non-stick baking paper in the fridge.

2 To cook, heat a little olive oil in a heavy-bottomed frying or grill pan set over a medium heat. Cook the koftas for about 15 minutes, turning regularly, until they feel slightly firm to the touch.

3 Transfer to a hot serving dish and sprinkle with very finely grated lemon zest. Serve immediately with the purslane salad and boiled new potatoes.

Salad of Purslane with Buttermilk Dressing, Chilli Oil, Roasted Hazelnuts and Cumin

150g purslane, gently washed and
dried, or rocket leaves
15–20g unskinned hazelnuts,
roasted, peeled and coarsely
chopped (see page 160-1 for
instructions on how to roast and
peel hazelnuts)
2 large pinches of roasted and
ground cumin seeds

Chilli oil
2 large fresh red chillies
140ml extra virgin olive oil
pinch of salt

Buttermilk dressing
150ml natural yogurt
50ml buttermilk
1 small garlic clove, peeled and
crushed to a paste
sea salt and freshly ground
black pepper

*At the times of the year when I don't have purslane, I replace it with rocket leaves or foraged wild greens. A mixture of wild watercress, wild garlic leaves and bittercress would be just lovely. I love the fact that all the elements for the salad dressing in this recipe – buttermilk, yogurt and garlic – are locally produced where I live. As the dairy-based dressing is heavier in weight compared to an oil-based dressing, I usually drizzle it over the leaves on the serving plate rather than tossing the leaves as I would with a lighter vinaigrette. This salad would also be good served alongside a bowl of almond hummus (page 160) and some crisp hot bread. **Serves 4-6***

1 To make the chilli oil, chop the chillies finely (including the seeds) and place in a very small saucepan with the olive oil and a pinch of salt. Bring to a **bare simmer** and cook at the gentlest bubble for 5 minutes, then remove from the heat. With the back of a spoon or a pestle, crush some of the chillies to break them up a little bit. Allow to cool completely, then strain through a fine sieve, again using the back of a spoon or a pestle to press some tiny bits of chilli flesh through. I try to get about 1 teaspoon of the fine flesh through the sieve into the oil. You can skip this stage of sieving if you wish and just serve the oil with the little pieces of chilli intact, but I find the oil to be somewhat more refined when I sieve it. Taste again and add another pinch of salt if necessary. Store in a cool place or in the fridge in a sealed glass container such as a jam jar. The oil will keep in the fridge for two weeks.

2 To make the dressing, mix the yogurt with the buttermilk and garlic and season lightly with salt and pepper.

3   Remove any long stalks from the purslane, chop
    them finely and spread out on a large flat serving
    dish. Drizzle on enough of the dressing to lightly
    coat the leaves. I use my fingers to gently tease
    the dressing through the leaves. Drizzle over 2–3
    tablespoons of chilli oil and scatter over the roasted
    hazelnuts. Finish the salad with the ground cumin
    dusted over the top and serve as soon as possible.

Peach Popsicles

700g ripe peaches

175g caster sugar

3 tablespoons lemon juice

To serve

langues de chat (page 168)

The issue with making homemade popsicles used to be the difficulty of getting the moulds and sticks, but that no longer seems to be a problem now that every kitchen shop in the country sells them.

There is something whimsical about eating an ice off a stick, and not just for younger people, as adults find them fun as well. When you combine the element of fun with something that is also really delicious, then you are on to a winner. The langues de chat biscuits on page 168 are a perfect accompaniment and seem to add to the retro nature of the experience.

Do buy your peaches a few days ahead to ensure that they are beautifully ripe and sweet.

I usually turn out the popsicles early in the day, wrap them in squares of parchment paper and return them to the freezer. The last thing you want to do is to have to rush this while surrounded by impatient children – and adults too, for that matter!

To make these into a more grown-up dessert you could serve them alongside glasses of sparkling wine for adults to dip the lollies into – delicious. **Makes 10–12**

1 Begin by peeling the peaches. With a small sharp knife, make a small cross in the top and bottom of the peaches and place in a deep bowl. Pour over **boiling water** and keep them immersed for **10 seconds**. Strain immediately and cool in a bowl of cold water for a minute or two. Drain again and peel off the skins, then slice the flesh off the stones. Discard the stones and place the flesh in a blender with the sugar and lemon juice. Purée until the fruit is smooth and silky and the sugar has dissolved. Fill into your popsicle moulds, pop a stick into the middle and freeze until completely frozen.

2 To serve, remove the popsicles from the freezer and allow to sit at room temperature until the popsicles slide easily out of the moulds. Keep a close eye on them to get the timing just right so that they don't become too soft. At this point I wrap the popsicles in small squares of parchment paper and refreeze them, ready for quick and easy serving later.

3 Serve the langues de chat separately. With a popsicle in one hand and a crisp biscuit in the other, all should be happy and content.

Autumn

The combination of beetroot and raspberries is not very well known or appreciated, but it really works. I have added some labneh to the mix, which is a simple yogurt cheese that is so easy to make. I am delighted when a cook discovers a technique that they thought was perhaps beyond them only to realise that it is simplicity itself. The dressing of olive oil, honey, lemon and mint draws all the flavours together. The dish has a smart, modern appearance and is equally beautiful when served in single servings as it is on a family-style platter.

I always think that quail or their eggs suggest a party or celebration of some sort, as they are such beautiful little creatures to look at and just as good to eat. The mild spice blend here complements the gentle, sweet flavour of the birds. I search for the new season walnuts that appear in autumn when making this dish. The flavour and creamy texture of the still-wet walnuts are fabulous. The combination of textures in the salad is lovely and I particularly like the salad leaf element, which keeps the dish light and fresh tasting.

The cake to finish this meal is a bit of a showstopper. The combination of lime and coconut is a popular one and this luscious cake showcases it very successfully. I usually serve it just as it is with whipped cream or crème fraîche, but in another meal I would serve a large bowl of fresh raspberries on the side as they work beautifully here. If you were desperate to serve raspberries with the cake, you could just omit them from the starter, which will still be delicious without them. I think it would be a mistake to serve the berries in two dishes in the same meal, but you make the rules in your house, so do as you see fit.

Beetroot and Autumn Raspberries with Honey, Mint and Labneh

2 medium beetroots, about 250g
   in total with tail and 3cm of stalk
   attached
sea salt and freshly ground
   black pepper
pinch of caster sugar
24 fresh raspberries
20 small fresh mint leaves

Labneh
500g full-fat natural yogurt
1 tablespoon extra virgin olive oil

Dressing
3 tablespoons extra virgin olive oil
1 tablespoon lemon juice
1 teaspoon honey

Beetroot and raspberries taste very good together and the labneh adds the savoury note. Labneh, a simple dripped yogurt cheese, is very easy to make, though you do need to start the process the previous day or at least early in the morning if you are serving it for dinner. There are many uses for labneh, and once you make it for the first time you will probably wonder why you never made it before. Search out full-fat thick organic yogurt for a rich and creamy result. **Serves 4**

1   To make the labneh, take a double thickness square of clean muslin or a fine linen glass cloth and place it over a sieve sitting over a bowl. Add the yogurt and olive oil and tie the four corners of the muslin to make a knot. Secure the knot with some string. You now need to hang the tied muslin bag by the string over the bowl to allow the whey in the yogurt to drip off for at least 8 hours, leaving you with a soft cheese. I hang the bag from a cup hook attached to a shelf and that works perfectly. If that all sounds too complicated, just sit the muslin bag in a sieve over a deep bowl and that also will do the job quite successfully. When the whey has all dripped out, simply remove the muslin and chill the cheese, covered, until you are ready to serve it. It will keep in the fridge for three or four days.

2   Rinse the beetroots under a cold running tap, being careful not to break off the little tail. Place in a saucepan and cover with cold water. Add a pinch of salt and sugar to the water. Bring to a simmer, cover and continue to simmer until the skin rubs off the beetroots easily when pushed. This can take anywhere from 30 minutes for fresh new season beetroots to 2 hours for older beets, so it is impossible to give an absolute time. The cooked beets should be very tender all the way through.

3 Peel off the skin and any remaining stalk and cut off the tail. The beets can be prepared up to this point hours ahead or even the previous day.

4 To make the dressing, whisk the olive oil, lemon juice, honey and some salt and pepper together. Taste and correct the seasoning.

5 To assemble the salad, slice the beetroots very thinly (I use a mandolin for this) and divide between four serving plates (the salad can also be assembled family style on a large flat platter and brought to the table). Cut some of the raspberries in half lengthways and some in cross-section slices and scatter over the beetroots. Whisk the dressing well and spoon some of it on. Place a dessertspoon of labneh in the centre of each plate. Scatter on the mint leaves and a final drizzle of dressing and serve.

Grilled Lightly Spiced Quail with Pomegranate and Walnut Salad

4 large quail
1 teaspoon coriander seeds
1 teaspoon cumin seeds
½ star anise
1 tablespoon extra virgin olive oil
zest and juice of 1 lemon

Salad

4 handfuls of mixed salad leaves
12 walnuts, cracked and
   nuts removed
2 tablespoons pomegranate seeds

Dressing

3 tablespoons walnut, hazelnut or
   extra virgin olive oil
1 tablespoon pomegranate molasses
sea salt and freshly ground
   black pepper

It is delightful to be able to use Irish quail, as there are several producers now rearing these little birds in this country. They always feel like a treat and the sweet, succulent flesh is delicious. Serve this salad on hot plates, otherwise the quail will cool too quickly and become greasy. I like to crack open walnuts from the shell when using them, as that way I am generally guaranteed a fresh, sweet nut. The pomegranate molasses used in the dressing is made from the juice of bitter pomegranates and adds a gentle sharpness to the dressing. **Serves 4**

1 Cut the quail in half by pushing your knife straight down through the breastbone.
2 Roast the coriander seeds, cumin seeds and star anise separately until lightly toasted. Grind to a coarse powder in a spice grinder or pestle and mortar.
3 Lay the quail halves in a flat dish and sprinkle on the ground spices, olive oil, lemon zest and juice and a pinch of sea salt. Turn the birds in the spicy oil and allow to marinate for at least 1 hour.
4 Wash and dry the salad leaves. Whisk together the walnut oil and pomegranate molasses for the dressing and season to taste with salt and pepper. Toss the walnuts and pomegranate seeds in 1 tablespoon of the dressing.
5 Heat a heavy-bottomed cast iron grill pan over a moderate heat until quite hot. Place the quail on the hot pan, breast side down, and grill until golden and the skin has crisped. Turn over and repeat the process on the other side. The quail will be in the pan for about 20 minutes in total. Keep a vigilant eye on the heat of the pan – you don't want it to cool down, but you also don't want to char the birds.
6 Divide the salad leaves, walnuts and pomegranate seeds between four hot plates. Snuggle two cooked quail halves into each salad and drizzle over the dressing. Serve immediately.

Toasted Coconut and Lime Cake

170g butter, softened, plus extra
   melted butter for greasing

150g caster sugar

1 teaspoon vanilla extract

3 eggs

170g self-raising flour

50g desiccated coconut

zest of 1 lime

2 tablespoons lime juice

Filling and icing

90g **cold** butter

175g icing sugar, sieved

110g cream cheese

zest of 1 lime

1 tablespoon lime juice

½ teaspoon vanilla extract

To finish

90g desiccated coconut

zest of 1 lime

To serve

softly whipped cream or
   crème fraîche

lime wedges

This is suitable for almost any occasion where a rich, delicious cake is required. The flavours are a bull's eye combination. I sometimes serve this cake with fresh raspberries, which is another flavour that works beautifully here. **Serves 8–10**

1 Preheat the oven to 180°C. Brush 2 x 20cm cake tins with a little melted butter and line the bottom of each tin with a disc of non-stick baking paper.

2 Place the butter in a large bowl and beat until it has paled in colour. Add the caster sugar and continue to beat until light and fluffy, then add the vanilla extract. Beat in the eggs one at a time, beating well between each addition. Sieve the flour over the eggs and butter and add the coconut and the lime zest and juice. Fold the ingredients together thoroughly but do not over-beat or you might make the cake tough.

3 Divide the batter between the prepared tins and bake in the oven for 20–25 minutes, until the cakes are well risen, a rich golden colour and feel somewhat spongy to the touch.

4 Remove from the oven and place on a wire rack, still in the tins. Allow to cool for 15 minutes, then gently remove from the tins and place on the wire rack to cool completely.

5 While the cakes are cooling, scatter the coconut over a baking tray in an even layer. Place in the oven until lightly toasted and golden. This takes about 10 minutes and **I usually stir the coconut once or twice to achieve an even colour**. Allow to cool completely.

6 To make the icing, place the butter in a food processor and blend to a creamy consistency. Add the remaining ingredients and blend again to achieve a smooth and spreadable icing.

7 To assemble, place one sponge on a flat plate and remove the paper disc. Spread on 2 tablespoons of the icing and pop on the other cake, paper disc removed, smooth side down. Cover the top and sides of the cake with the remaining icing. A palette knife works well for this purpose. Dust the top and sides of the cake with the toasted coconut and sprinkle the lime zest over the top of the cake. It may look like you have too much toasted coconut, but keep pressing it gently onto the side and top of the cake and you will end up using it all.

8 I serve the cake with softly whipped cream or crème fraîche and a little plate of lime wedges on the side.

I have always loved the classic Italian tonnato sauce made with tinned tuna, but this version made with smoked mackerel is a discovery I am very pleased with. It came about one day when I did not have any tuna to hand and the smoked mackerel was staring out of the fridge at me, and I thought, well, why not? Vine-ripened heritage tomatoes and sweet basil are perfect with the smoked fish and the egg adds a richness to complete a very satisfying dish. The presentation is easy and good bread is the ideal accompaniment. This dish is a starter here, but it would make a sustaining and nourishing lunch or supper when accompanied by a bowl of hot boiled new potatoes (page 38).

The technique used to butterfly the chicken to create a paillard for the main course in this meal is quite simple. You simply slice into one side of the chicken breast, cutting towards the centre to open the breast out to look somewhat like a butterfly. The advantage of this process, apart from the lovely visual effect, is that you have doubled the surface area of the chicken on which you can build up cooking colour to add flavour and texture. The roasted grapes to accompany the grilled meat are simple and full of good taste. The roasted almonds and rosemary marry all the flavours together and the whole dish looks terrific when the simple elements are presented together.

I serve big bowls of simple boiled potatoes and green cabbage as the vegetables in this meal and they are perfect with the chicken.

The tart to finish this meal is a real surprise. Many people feel the same way about dates as they do about prunes – they just do not love them. However, I have witnessed this tart changing guests' opinion about this immensely important fruit. The dates and vanilla are set in a rich custard to create a delicate and delicious confection. Big fat Medjool dates are ideal here and their sweetness and meatiness are a revelation in the creamy, vanilla-flecked filling. This tart is best served slightly warm with chilly softly whipped cream on the side. This is one of my absolute favourite sweet tarts.

Smoked Mackerel 'Tonnato' with Heritage Tomatoes, Basil and a Hen's Egg

6 eggs

6 teaspoons capers

6 tinned anchovy fillets, chopped

6 ripe heritage tomatoes, sliced

sea salt and freshly ground
black pepper

6 large fresh basil leaves, plus extra
for garnish

4 tablespoons extra virgin olive oil

pinch of caster sugar

120g smoked mackerel,
skin removed

Smoked mackerel 'tonnato'

150g homemade mayonnaise
(page 258)

25g smoked mackerel, skin removed

1–2 tablespoons water

a few drops of lemon juice

The classic tonnato sauce is of course made with tuna, but here I have used smoked mackerel and I think it is just as good. The sweet vine-ripened summer tomatoes and fragrant basil complement the smoked fish brilliantly. **Serves 6**

1   Hard-boil the eggs by lowering them gently into a saucepan of **boiling salted water** and cooking them at a boil for exactly 10 minutes. If you don't want the yolk to be completely hard, cook for 9 minutes. The salt in the water seasons the egg and will help to coagulate any white that might seep out of a crack in the shell, hence less leakage. Remove from the saucepan immediately with a slotted spoon and cool under a cold running tap. Remove the shell and cut the hard-boiled eggs in half or into quarters.

2   To make the 'tonnato', place the mayonnaise and smoked mackerel in a food processor and blend to a purée. Add enough water to achieve a soft, spreadable consistency. Taste and add a few drops of lemon juice to brighten up the flavour.

3   To assemble, spread 1 tablespoon of the mackerel 'tonnato' in a wide circle on flat plates. Scatter each circle with 1 teaspoon of capers and an equal portion of chopped anchovy.

4   Place the sliced tomatoes in a single layer on another flat plate and season with salt and pepper. Tear over the basil leaves and dress immediately with the olive oil. Tease the dressing and basil through the tomatoes with your fingers. Taste one piece of tomato – if it is underwhelming, add a pinch of sugar and perhaps a little more salt to lift the flavour.

5   Divide the tomatoes and any oily juices between the plates. Tear the mackerel into pieces and scatter it through the tomatoes. Add the halved or quartered hard-boiled eggs to each plate. Garnish each plate with a few more basil leaves and serve.

Chicken Paillard with Roasted Grapes and Almonds

2 large chicken breasts, skin on

6 tablespoons extra virgin olive oil

sea salt and freshly ground
   black pepper

450g grapes, cut into little bunches
   of about 6 grapes

a few sprigs of fresh thyme

2 tablespoons lemon juice

1 tablespoon chopped
   fresh rosemary

2 tablespoons whole unskinned
   almonds

To serve

boiled cabbage (page 154)

boiled new potatoes (page 38)

The technique of butterflying a chicken breast to create a paillard is really simple and results in twice the surface area on the chicken for lots of extra colour and flavour. Cooking grapes to serve with savoury food may seem like a novel idea, but here the roasted grapes are delicious when combined with the sweet chicken, crisp almonds and rosemary. The juices that escape from the cooked grapes mixed with the olive oil make a light sauce for the dish. Look out for home-grown grapes in the autumn, which generally have a wonderful flavour, but especially the Muscat variety, which is a particular favourite of mine. **Serves 4**

1 Preheat the oven to 200°C.

2 Remove the fillets from the chicken breasts and reserve. Place one of the chicken breasts on a board, skin side down. Cut into the chicken breast from top to bottom, leaving it hinged on one side so that you can open it out like a book. If the opened-out breast looks a little uneven, just flatten it with the back of your knife. Repeat with the other breast. Place the breasts and fillets in a bowl with **2 tablespoons of the olive oil** and season with salt and pepper. Mix gently to coat the chicken in the olive oil and seasoning.

3 Place the grapes in a bowl with the thyme sprigs, the remaining **4 tablespoons of olive oil**, salt and pepper and mix gently. Transfer to a small roasting tray that holds the grapes snugly and roast in the oven for about 40 minutes. **If the roasting tray is too big, the olive oil and grape juices will burn.** The cooked grapes should be lovely and tender but still holding their shape.

4 Remove from the oven and add the lemon juice and rosemary. At this point I usually squash a few of the grapes to release their juices into the oil. This almost makes a warm vinaigrette for dressing the chicken. I leave the thyme sprigs with the grapes and they become part of the presentation. Cover the grapes and keep warm.

5 Roast the almonds on a dry baking tray in the same oven as the grapes for about 10 minutes, until crisp and well coloured. Remove and allow to cool a little, then chop coarsely. The grapes and almonds can be prepared ahead of time to this point. If necessary, the grapes can be popped back into a hot oven to reheat later.

6 Preheat a heavy grill pan over a moderate heat until the **pan is hot**. Place the chicken pieces on the pan, **skin side down**. The chicken should **sizzle** the moment it hits the pan. If it does not, remove it immediately and wait for the pan to be properly hot. Allow the chicken to become golden brown on the skin side. This will take about 10 minutes and you will need to keep an eye on the temperature of the pan to maintain a hot but not blistering heat. **Resist the temptation to move or turn the chicken before it is properly coloured and the skin is crisp.** As the skin and flesh cook and colour, it almost lifts off the pan and should no longer be difficult to turn. Cook on the other side for about another 8 minutes, until the chicken feels firm to the touch and the juices run clear. When the chicken is cooked, I like to rest it for 5 minutes or longer in a low oven set at 100°C. I place the cooked meat on an upside-down small plate sitting on top of a bigger plate. Any juices that run out of the resting chicken are saved in the larger plate.

7   To serve, divide the bunches of grapes and thyme sprigs between hot plates. At this point the thyme sprigs will be looking a little skeletal, which I like. If that is not to your liking, just discard them. Carve the breasts in half and put on the plates with the chicken fillets added to the plates of the bigger eaters. Scatter the almonds all over the plates. **Quickly reheat the juices** from the grape roasting tray along with any juices from the chicken resting plate to a simmer and spoon over. Serve immediately with bowls of boiled cabbage and boiled new potatoes on the side.

Boiled Cabbage

1 head of cabbage, such as Savoy
sea salt and freshly ground
 black pepper
butter or extra virgin olive oil

Cabbage is highly underrated and undervalued. It is tremendously good value for money and there is almost always a variety that is in season at all times of the year.

There are many good varieties of cabbage, but I particularly like the crinkly green leaves of the Savoy cabbage. I also love the elegant shape of Greyhound cabbage, so called because the head looks like the long, elegant nose of a greyhound. Dark green spring cabbage is also a favourite. I avoid the densely tight white cabbages, except perhaps for a coleslaw, though I am always more likely to reach for a head of green cabbage, regardless of the recipe that I am making. **Serves 4–6**

1 Remove any damaged outer leaves from the cabbage, but don't remove any more of the nice green outside leaves than is necessary, as they are full of flavour. Place the cabbage on a chopping board and cut directly down through the middle of the head, then quarter the cabbage and remove the hard core. Thinly **slice the cabbage against the grain**.

2 Bring about 1.75 litres of water to a rolling boil and salt it well. Add the cabbage and simmer, **uncovered**, until the cabbage is tender, which should take about 10 minutes. Strain off the cooking water.

3 If you wish you can now toss the cabbage in a little butter or olive oil and give it a few twists of the black pepper mill.

Medjool Date and Vanilla Tart

15 Medjool dates, halved lengthways
   and stones removed
6 egg yolks
85g caster sugar
½ vanilla pod
600ml cream

Pastry
110g cold butter, diced
220g plain flour
25g caster sugar
1 egg
a few drops of water
a little beaten egg

To serve
softly whipped cream

This is a delectable tart. The combination of date, vanilla and cream is quite delicious, and even avowed date haters have been convinced by this. I like it best served slightly warm, but it is still really good the next day served at room temperature.
Serves 8

1 For the pastry, rub the butter into the flour either by hand or using a food processor to achieve a fine crumb. If using a food processor, transfer the mixture to a bowl and add the sugar. Beat the egg and add to the flour with a fork, adding a few drops of water if necessary to bring the pastry together. Knead the pastry just enough to achieve a smooth mass. Form into a neat flat disc, cover and chill in the fridge for at least 30 minutes.

2 Roll the pastry on a lightly floured surface and line a deep 23cm flan tin with a loose base with it. Try to achieve a slightly raised pastry edge a few millimetres proud of the top of the flan tin. Chill for 30 minutes.

3 Preheat the oven to 180°C.

4 Line the tart shell with parchment or greaseproof paper and fill to the very top with dried beans. Bake in the oven for 20 minutes, then remove the paper and beans and paint the base of the tart with a little beaten egg to seal it. Return to the oven and cook for a further 10 minutes, until the pastry looks golden and just cooked. Remove from the oven and allow to cool a little before assembling the tart.

5 Place the halved and stoned dates on the pastry in circles with the cut side uppermost.

6 Cream the egg yolks and sugar until light and fluffy. Cut the vanilla pod in half lengthways. With the blunt side of a knife, scrape out the seeds and add to the mixture. Stir in the cream and mix gently but thoroughly. Gently pour the cream over

the dates, being careful not to dislodge them. The filling will come right up to cover the dates.

7 Bake in the oven for about 90 minutes, until just set. If you think the tart is colouring too much, lay a sheet of parchment paper over the tart once the skin on top has set. I like the top of the tart to be well coloured, somewhat like the colour of a roasted hazelnut.

8 Once the tart is gently but definitely set, remove from the oven and place on a wire rack to cool. Serve warm or at room temperature with softly whipped cream.

The addition of roasted almonds to the chickpeas in this hummus is very pleasant and I think that the entire dish makes a fulfilling starter. You need to be a bit brave when seasoning and adding the lemon juice to the hummus, as if it is not accurately seasoned it can be somewhat bland. The late additions of the smoked paprika oil, pumpkin seeds, roasted hazelnuts and lemon zest are the vital finishing seasonings that really make the dish sing. I love a soft and creamy consistency to the finished purée. The dish looks wonderful on a large wide dish when everyone can draw the vegetables through the hummus while catching seeds, nuts and deeply coloured paprika oil at the same time.

I think the simple grilled spring onions in the main course in this meal is perhaps one of the most useful recipes in this book. It is certainly one of the easiest. The combination of the slightly charred spring onions, mushrooms and anchovy is deeply satisfying and the egg and crispy pangrattato complete what is for me a perfect meat-free dish. The utterly easy spring onions on their own are terrific with almost all roast or grilled meat, poultry or fish and I am somewhat obsessed with them. It is thrilling in the kitchen when sometimes the easiest dish is such a winner, so don't forget to use the recipe whenever you want a deep grilled or roasted onion flavour.

The presentation of the chocolate and caramel whip is somewhat retro due to the fact that it is pushed through a piping bag fitted with a star-shaped nozzle. No apologies from me, though, as I think it looks great. The most important thing, of course, is that the whip tastes good, and it does. The langues de chat add to the fun nature of the presentation.

Roasted Almond Hummus with Roasted Carrots, Beetroot, Hazelnuts and Pumpkin Seeds

175g dried chickpeas

100g unskinned almonds

150g tahini

2 garlic cloves, peeled and crushed
   to a paste

juice of 1 lemon

2 tablespoons extra virgin olive oil

1½ teaspoons cumin seeds, toasted
   and ground

200ml chickpea cooking water

sea salt and freshly ground
   black pepper

Vegetables

8 carrots, peeled and cut in half
   lengthways

4 small beetroots, quartered

2 branches of fresh thyme

2 tablespoons extra virgin olive oil

To finish

25g unskinned hazelnuts

1 tablespoon extra virgin olive oil

1 teaspoon smoked paprika

2 tablespoons pumpkin seeds,
   toasted

zest of 1 lemon

I serve this variation of a classic chickpea hummus here with roasted carrots and beetroot, but I make it year round and vary the vegetables according to the season. Raw green vegetables such as courgettes or cucumbers are good, as are radishes, spring onions, broccolis, kale leaves and watercress. On another day in another meal the entire dish would make the perfect accompaniment for a roast leg of lamb with bubbling hot gravy and a mint sauce. **Serves 8**

1 Place the chickpeas in a large bowl, cover with plenty of cold water and soak overnight.

2 The next day, preheat the oven to 200°C.

3 Strain and discard the chickpea soaking water. Place the chickpeas in a saucepan, cover with **fresh cold water** and bring to a simmer. Cover and cook gently until the peas are cooked. The cooking time can vary from 30 to 60 minutes and will depend on the size and age of the chickpeas, but they need to be completely tender if you want to achieve a smooth, creamy hummus. Keep an eye on the water level in the saucepan and if necessary top it up to keep the chickpeas submerged. When the chickpeas are cooked, strain and **reserve 200ml of the cooking water**. Allow the chickpeas to cool.

4 Meanwhile, roast the almonds in the oven on a dry baking tray until crisp and well coloured. This should take about 10 minutes.

5 Toss the carrots and beetroot with the thyme, olive oil and some salt and pepper. Place in a single layer on a roasting tray and roast in the oven for about 30 minutes, until well coloured and tender. Keep warm.

6 When the vegetables come out of the oven, **reduce the temperature to 180°C**. Place the hazelnuts on a baking tray and roast in the oven for about 15 minutes, until the skins are starting to lift and flake

and the nuts are golden brown. Remove the tray from the oven and allow the nuts to cool. Place the cold nuts in a clean kitchen towel, gather up the edges of the towel and rub the base of the towel on the palm of your hand to loosen the skins as much as possible. You will not get every last piece of skin off, but that's fine. Coarsely chop the roasted nuts and reserve for later.

7 Place the cooled chickpeas and the roasted almonds in a food processer and purée for a moment or two. Add the tahini, garlic, lemon juice, olive oil, cumin and three-quarters of the chickpea cooking water and purée again **until the hummus is smooth. If it is a little dry, add the remaining cooking water in increments.** Taste and correct the seasoning.

8 Mix the olive oil and smoked paprika together in a small bowl.

9 To serve, spread the hummus on plates and place the roasted vegetables on top. Drizzle with the smoked paprika oil. Sprinkle each plate with some roasted hazelnuts, toasted pumpkin seeds and lemon zest and a final pinch of sea salt.

Grilled Spring Onions with Mushrooms, Anchovy, Hen's Egg and Pangratatto

4 eggs

24 fat spring onions, trimmed of any tired outside leaves (leave the root end on)

4 tablespoons extra virgin olive oil

sea salt and freshly ground black pepper

180g flat mushrooms, coarsely chopped

1 teaspoon fresh thyme leaves

8 anchovies, **4 chopped and 4 left whole**

1 tablespoon water

best-quality extra virgin olive oil, for drizzling

Pangrattato

50g coarse sourdough breadcrumbs

½ tablespoon extra virgin olive oil

You will need to be brave when grilling the spring onions, as it is crucial to leave them under the grill long enough for them to both tenderise and colour sufficiently. I like the green ends of some of the spring onions to be cooked until quite charred. As this dish is being served as a main course in this meal, I have allowed one egg per serving. If you would like to serve this as a lunch or supper dish, you could serve half an egg per person. Instead of the hard-boiled egg suggested here I sometimes served a soft poached egg, and that is very good too. **Serves 4**

1   Preheat the grill element in your oven, or failing that, preheat the oven to the highest heat possible, although the direct heat of the grill produces the best result.

2   While the grill is heating up, hard-boil the eggs by lowering them gently into a saucepan of **boiling salted water** and cooking them at a boil for exactly 10 minutes. If you don't want the yolk to be completely hard, cook for 9 minutes. The salt in the water seasons the egg and will help to coagulate any white that might seep out of a crack in the shell, hence less leakage. Remove from the saucepan immediately with a slotted spoon and cool under a cold running tap. Remove the shell and cut the hard-boiled eggs in half lengthways.

3   Toss the spring onions in 2 tablespoons of the olive oil and season with salt and pepper. Place in a single layer on a baking sheet and place under the hot grill. Cook them until completely tender, by which time some of the spring onion ends will have become slightly charred. This is crucial for the finished flavour of the dish. This takes about 7 minutes under my grill and it might take longer in yours, but it is unlikely to take less time. **I turn them with a tongs three or four times** during the cooking to ensure a good result.

When the spring onions are sufficiently tender and coloured, remove from the sheet and allow to cool to room temperature, though they are also very good served warm.

4 To make the pangrattato, toss the breadcrumbs in the olive oil and spread in an even layer on the sheet the spring onions were cooked on. Place under the grill or in the hot oven and allow to become crisp and coloured to a hazelnut shade. This should only take a matter of minutes. I usually turn them once or twice during the cooking. **Be vigilant here, as they will crisp and colour quickly.** Once ready, remove from the oven and set aside.

5 Heat 1 tablespoon of the olive oil in a frying pan set over a moderate heat and add the mushrooms and thyme leaves. Season with salt and pepper and fry for about 8 minutes, until juicy and cooked. Tip them into a food processor along with any cooking juices and allow to cool slightly for 5 minutes, then add the **chopped anchovies** and blend. Add the remaining tablespoon of oil and the water and blend again to make a purée, but it does not need to be completely smooth. Taste and correct the seasoning.

6 To assemble the dish, place a knot of six spring onions on each plate. Place a dessertspoon of the mushroom purée on top, followed by a hard-boiled egg cut in half lengthways and a **whole anchovy**. Sprinkle over some pangrattato and finish with a small drizzle of excellent olive oil.

Chocolate and Caramel Whip with Langues de Chat

225g caster or granulated sugar

250ml cream

150g chocolate (at least 52% cocoa
   solids), chopped into small pieces

1 teaspoon vanilla extract

pinch of salt

250ml whipped cream (measured
   after whipping)

To serve

langues de chat (page 168)

fresh raspberries, when in season

I make a chocolate and caramel mousse that is a good deal richer and more complicated than this recipe, so I am calling this a whip partly to differentiate it from my other recipe but also because this can be pushed through a piping bag for its final presentation, in which case it resembles a chocolate whip. Caramel and chocolate is such a good combination of flavours and this is easy to make. I serve pistachio-topped langues de chat as a crisp biscuit alongside. Fresh raspberries when in season also make a perfect accompaniment. **Serves 8**

1 Place the sugar in a deep heavy-bottomed saucepan and cook over a moderate heat until it is a chestnut-coloured caramel, which should take about 8 minutes. You will need to stir the sugar at intervals to encourage it to cook evenly. At various stages during the cooking it may look lumpy and unlikely to ever become smooth, but **keep the faith** and keep stirring and **it will eventually become smooth just as it reaches the colour of a chestnut caramel**.

2 Once the chestnut caramel has been achieved, pull the saucepan off the heat and add the cream. Be careful, as it will splutter, so you may need to add the cream gradually. Stir the saucepan with a flat-bottomed wooden spoon to encourage the cream and caramel to mix. If the caramel is not completely dissolving, put the saucepan on a low heat and return to a simmer.

3 **Allow to cool for 5 minutes**, then add the chocolate and vanilla and stir continuously to melt the chocolate into the sauce. Add a small pinch of salt. Allow to cool, then **chill until completely cold**.

4 When cold, fold in the whipped cream thoroughly. The consistency of the firm chocolate and soft cream are quite different, so it usually takes a few minutes to blend the two. **Once blended I usually**

whisk it by hand for a moment or two to firm it up to a piping consistency. Using a piping bag fitted with a medium or large star-shaped nozzle, pipe the mixture into your serving dishes of choice.

5   The whip is now ready to serve with the biscuits and fresh raspberries (or your accompaniment of choice) or it can be covered and returned to the fridge, tightly covered, for up to 24 hours for serving later.

Langues de Chat

125g butter, at room temperature

125g caster sugar

175g plain flour, sieved

4 egg whites

¼ teaspoon vanilla extract

4 tablespoons finely chopped
   pistachio nuts (optional)

*These thin biscuits are so called because they are supposed to resemble the shape of cats' tongues. I like to shape these into long, skinny biscuits, perhaps more like a lizard's tongue, but that name would not sell them very well! Regardless of the length, they should be quite thin and delicate. I serve them with mousses, fools, soufflés, ices of all sorts and of course with a cup of tea or coffee. The flavouring here is vanilla, but orange or lemon zest or ground sweet spices such as cinnamon or star anise also work well. Finely chopped nuts such as pistachios, almonds, pecans or Brazil nuts can be scattered over the shaped and uncooked batter to give a crunchy and flavoursome finish. **Serves 8***

1 Preheat the oven to 180°C. Line a flat baking tray with non-stick baking paper.
2 Place the butter and sugar in a mixing bowl and beat vigorously until pale and fluffy.
3 Add the sieved flour, unwhisked egg whites and vanilla extract and fold gently with a spatula until the mixture is combined. It will look like a thick batter.
4 Transfer the mixture into a piping bag fitted with a 1cm nozzle or use a disposable plastic piping bag and just snip off the top with a scissors to give exactly the size needed. I wash and dry the bag and keep it for the next time. Pipe onto the lined baking tray in long, thin rows 1cm thick and 10cm long. Leave a 3cm gap between the biscuits to allow them to spread a little when cooking. If you are using the pistachio nuts, sprinkle them onto the uncooked biscuits now.
5 Bake in the oven for 12 minutes, by which time they will have coloured generously around the edges. Remove from the oven and allow to cool on the baking tray. When cool, remove to a wire rack and store in an airtight box lined with kitchen paper for up to 48 hours.

MEAL 4

–

Chilled Cucumber and Grape
Soup with Elderflower,
Pomegranate and Mint

–

Fried Spiced Chicken with
Tomato Aioli and Salsa Cruda

–

Tuscan Dessert Apple, Lemon
and Almond Cake

Although a chilled soup is generally associated with the warmer times of the year, I actually serve them year round. This pretty, fresh-tasting soup is the perfect way to start this meal, as its cooling nature is a good foil for the crisp spiced chicken that follows. Each mouthful here should yield lovely tastes and textures, with the unsweetened yogurt at the base of it all. The soup can be made several hours ahead and chilled, then the final garnish of sliced radishes, pomegranate seeds and flower petals can be added just before serving so that the soup arrives to the table looking like a little jewelled garden.

Crispy fried chicken has always been a personal favourite and the spiced flour in this recipe adds a tingling kick of heat to the crunch of the chicken skin. The garlic- and tomato-flavoured aioli is a terrific sauce that I also serve with crisp fried fish. A spicy, freshly made salsa of firm, ripe tomatoes, hot chilli and crisp salad leaves brings the whole dish together. I usually don't serve cutlery with this dish, but rather encourage diners to dip their crispy drumsticks into their own dipping bowl of aioli and the salsa is served in little boat-shaped crisp lettuce leaves for an easy pick-up. I do put little finger bowls on the table, though, as by the time everyone has eaten their fill, hands tend to be a bit sticky. But if you think that is all too much of a palaver, just use cutlery after all.

After the rather hands-on main course, things calm down again as this meal finishes with a simple apple cake from Italy. Sweet dessert apples are cooked in a light almond sponge and finished with an apricot glaze to give it a gorgeous shine. If you have them, a sprinkling of finely chopped fresh geranium leaves is a pretty and scented final flourish, but this cake is really worth making with or without the geranium leaves.

Chilled Cucumber and Grape Soup with Elderflower, Pomegranate and Mint

350g cucumber, unpeeled and
   coarsely grated

150g seedless grapes, sliced, or
   seeded grapes, halved and seeds
   removed

250ml natural yogurt

100ml apple juice

2–3 tablespoons elderflower cordial

2 tablespoons finely chopped
   fresh mint

sea salt and freshly ground
   black pepper

6 radishes, thinly sliced

6 tablespoons pomegranate seeds

fresh edible flower petals, such as
   rose, marigold, viola or chive,
   to garnish

This chilled soup is full of delicious flavours and textures and it looks very pretty with the final garnish of pomegranate seeds, radishes and flower petals. I leave the skin on the cucumber as I like the flavour and I use an old-fashioned coarse grater to achieve a somewhat robust texture. **Serves 6**

1 Mix the cucumber, grapes, yogurt, apple juice, elderflower cordial, mint and some salt and pepper together. Taste and correct the seasoning. Chill for at least 1 hour.

2 To serve, divide the soup between six bowls and garnish each serving with sliced radishes, a generous sprinkling of pomegranate seeds and flower petals (if using). Serve immediately.

Fried Spiced Chicken with Tomato Aioli and Salsa Cruda

1 litre chicken stock (page 257)

12–16 small chicken drumsticks or a mixture of drumsticks and thighs, all on the bone

1 litre sunflower oil, for deep frying

250ml buttermilk, for dipping the chicken in

Spiced flour

150g plain flour

3 tablespoons white sesame seeds

4 teaspoons ground white pepper

4 teaspoons chilli powder

4 teaspoons curry powder

large pinch of fine sea salt

To serve

20–30 small crisp lettuce leaves, such as cos or baby gem

fresh coriander leaves

tomato aioli (page 175)

salsa cruda (page 178)

*Fried chicken can be one of the most delicious and satisfying things to eat. I love the little bit of heat in the spiced flour here. The aioli is somewhat rich, but it pairs beautifully with the crisp chicken. I serve the salsa in small crisp lettuce leaves drizzled with the aioli, which makes them easy to pick up, just like the chicken. You won't need cutlery here, as the only way to eat fried chicken is with your fingers. Purists will wonder why I have not soaked the chicken pieces in buttermilk before cooking, but in this highly flavoured recipe, I don't find it to be necessary. **Serves 6–8***

1 Place the chicken stock in a saucepan that the chicken pieces will fit into snugly and bring to a simmer. Add the chicken and season with a pinch of salt. Cover the saucepan with a lid and simmer very gently until the chicken is tender and cooked through. This will take about 1 hour. Remove the chicken from the stock and allow to cool. **Reserve the stock**, which will be deliciously flavoured for adding to the aioli.

2 Preheat the oven to 160°C.

3 Mix all the spiced flour ingredients in a bowl.

4 When you are ready to fry the chicken, heat 10cm of sunflower oil in a deep frier or heavy-bottomed cast iron or stainless steel saucepan until it reaches 180°C. Dip the chicken pieces in the buttermilk and massage the milk onto the skin thoroughly. Shake off the excess milk and dust the chicken pieces thoroughly with the spiced flour.

5 Drop the chicken gently into the hot oil, which should **sizzle on contact** with the chicken. **Don't over-fill the pan** or the temperature of the oil will drop and the chicken pieces will stew rather than fry. A long-handled tongs is the best piece of equipment to use now, as you will also need to turn the chicken pieces every now and then to get

them to colour and crisp evenly. Remember, the chicken is already cooked, so you are just reheating the pieces and also of course trying to achieve the perfect **golden colour and crisp texture**. Remove the pieces from the oil and drain on kitchen paper. Keep them hot in the oven and continue frying until all the pieces are crisp and golden.

6 Serve the hot chicken with the crisp lettuce leaves, coriander leaves and aioli and salsa on the side. I sometimes pile a little salsa onto the salad leaves, drizzle with some aioli and finish with coriander leaves – this makes the eating a little easier for my guests.

Tomato Aioli

2 egg yolks

2 anchovies, finely chopped

1 tablespoon thick tomato purée

2 teaspoons finely chopped garlic

1 teaspoon white wine vinegar

1 teaspoon Dijon mustard

125ml sunflower oil

100ml extra virgin olive oil

50–75ml chicken poaching liquid
    from the fried chicken on page 173

3 tablespoons chopped
    fresh coriander

sea salt and freshly ground
    black pepper

lemon juice, to taste

This sauce is perfect with the fried chicken, but I also serve it with fried fish. In that case, I also accompany it with the tomato salsa on page 178, as suggested in this dish. **Serves 6–8**

Place the egg yolks, anchovies, tomato purée, garlic, vinegar and mustard in a food processor. With the machine running, slowly pour in the oils, as if making a mayonnaise, and process until smooth. Now add just enough of the chicken poaching liquid to attain a coating consistency. Stir in the coriander by hand and taste the aioli, correcting the seasoning with salt and pepper and perhaps a few drops of lemon juice.

Pumpkin Soup with
Herb Oil and Crisped
Pumpkin Seeds, *p183*

Fried Spiced Chicken, with Tomato Aioli and Salsa Cruda, *p173*

Lime Oreos, *p193*

Salsa Cruda

4 firm, ripe, unpeeled tomatoes,
cut into 1cm dice

1 small red onion, peeled and
finely chopped

1–2 medium-hot fresh chillies,
deseeded and finely chopped

1 large garlic clove, peeled and
crushed to a paste

1 tablespoon finely chopped fresh
coriander leaves

1 tablespoon lime juice

pinch of caster sugar

*Depending on how much chilli you add, you can make the
salsa as hot or as mild as you wish, though I like to serve it
with a reasonable kick of heat.* **Serves 6–8**

Simply mix all the salsa ingredients together, then
taste and correct the seasoning. I like to eat this salsa
on the day it's made.

Tuscan Dessert Apple, Lemon and Almond Cake

4 dessert apples

finely grated zest of 2 lemons

250g + 1 dessertspoon caster sugar

2 eggs

1 teaspoon vanilla extract

150ml cream

110g butter, melted and cooled, plus
   extra for greasing

125g whole almonds, blanched,
   peeled and ground to a fine
   powder in a food processer, or
   ground almonds

110g plain flour, sieved

1½ teaspoons baking powder, sieved

Apricot glaze

100g apricot jam

1 tablespoon lemon juice

To finish

2 tablespoons chopped sweet
   geranium leaves (optional)

softly whipped cream

I am never quite sure if I should be calling this a cake or a tart, but in any event it is delicious and quite easy to make. The origins of the recipe are from Tuscany in Italy, but I like to use highly perfumed Irish dessert apples when in season. Look out for some lesser-known Irish dessert apples, such as Irish Peach and Ard Cairn Russet. **Serves 8**

1 Preheat the oven to 180°C. Line a 28cm flan ring with a removable base with a disc of non-stick baking paper. The paper should be in one piece and it should cover the base and sides of the tin and **come 1cm above the edge of the tin**. Brush the paper with a little melted butter.

2 Peel, core and quarter the apples, then cut into slices about 3mm thick. Mix with the lemon zest.

3 Whisk the 250g of sugar with the eggs and vanilla to a thick, light consistency similar to a batter. Whisk in the cream and cooled melted butter. Fold in the ground almonds, flour and baking powder. Add **three-quarters of the sliced apples**, being careful not to break up the apple slices.

4 Pour the mixture into the prepared flan ring and gently smooth the surface. **Scatter the remaining apples** over the surface and sprinkle with the dessertspoon of caster sugar.

5 Bake in the oven for 20 minutes, then reduce the temperature to 160°C and cook for a further 40 minutes, by which time the tart will feel gently set. It may be necessary to cover the tart during the cooking time with a sheet of non-stick baking paper if the tart is getting too dark. Remove from the oven and allow to cool slightly.

6 While the tart is cooling, make the apricot glaze. Warm the apricot jam and lemon juice in a small saucepan to just soften the jam.

Don't allow it to boil or it will dull the flavour. Pass through a fine sieve, pushing through as much as you can.

7 While the tart is still warm, paint the surface with the apricot glaze to achieve a shiny finish. If using the chopped geranium, sprinkle it on immediately after glazing the tart. Serve warm with softly whipped cream.

This would be a good Halloween meal, with both seasonal ingredients and flavours.

Pumpkins and squash, once an unusual sight here, are now widely available. What used to be seen as something rather exotic is now better understood and there are many growers producing lots of varieties, both for eating and for the annual Halloween display. Understanding that some varieties make better decoration than eating is very important when you choose one to cook with. You want a firm-fleshed variety here with a deep colour, as that saturation of colour is generally reflected in the flavour. My favourite pumpkin is the Red Kuri, but I also really like butternut squash. Either will make a highly flavoured soup with a super-silky consistency. This soup looks especially attractive when served with a glistening slick of herb oil and the crisp pumpkin seeds.

In springtime I add very little to my delicate lamb other than salt and pepper, but as the year progresses I can ramp up the flavourings as the flavour of the meat itself becomes more robust. The braised lamb here is a curious mix of herbs and spices, but the flavours are really delicious with a slight hint of India from the curry powder mix. Curry powder varies enormously and many of them are too strong and not well balanced. Search out a good one or else use my recipe on page 258 to make your own. Rice would seem like the perfect accompaniment to the spiced lamb, but I actually prefer a creamy mashed potato. I would almost certainly serve a green vegetable too, and given the time of year, I think it would be my good friend the green cabbage cooked in plenty of boiling salted water (page 154).

I suppose I am taking a bit of liberty here calling the biscuits to finish this meal Oreos, the much-loved American cookie, but they are great fun and I think they are pretty good. The addition of lime cuts through the sweetness and adds a freshness that I like. They can be served on their own, but with the yogurt and banana ice they become rather grown up and will amuse all.

Pumpkin Soup with Herb Oil and Crisped Pumpkin Seeds

50g butter or 4 tablespoons extra
   virgin olive oil

450g pumpkin or butternut squash
   (weight after peeling), peeled and
   cut into 2cm dice

225g onions, peeled and sliced

4 garlic cloves, peeled and crushed
   to a paste

sea salt and freshly ground
   black pepper

1.2 litres chicken stock (page 257)

225ml creamy milk (optional)

To garnish

herb oil (page 186)

4 tablespoons pumpkin seeds,
   toasted on a dry pan until crisp

This is a very simple recipe, but I think it shows off the flavour and silky consistency of the pumpkin rather perfectly. The soup can be garnished with many different ingredients, ranging from a simple swirl of cream or a drizzle of olive oil to a wide range of complementary fresh herbs such as thyme, rosemary or marjoram. The final flourish in this case is herb oil with a little chilli to add some heat and a scattering of crisp pumpkin seeds.

The variety of pumpkins available seems to grow every year and it can be a challenge to decide which one is the best to use. A selection of pumpkins at your vegetable shop or local farmers market is a glorious sight. Varied in colour, size and shape, it is definitely an autumnal scene and a treat for the eye. Avoid the varieties that have been grown solely for carving into scary Halloween faces, as they are watery and have a dull flavour. For this soup I like to use the variety called Uchiki Kuri, Red Kuri or Japanese pumpkin. It has a shape like a cannonball, is a deep joyful orange colour and has quite a hard skin. Butternut squash is also an excellent alternative to the pumpkin here.

Be careful when peeling the pumpkin, as the skin can be tough and can cause your knife to slip, so make sure your knife is always pointing away from you when you are preparing the vegetable. **Serves 6–8**

1   Melt the butter or heat the oil in a saucepan set over a moderate heat. Allow the butter to foam or the oil to get quite hot. Add the pumpkin, onions and garlic. Season with salt and pepper and coat the vegetables in the fat. Cover with a butter wrapper or a piece of greaseproof paper and the lid of the saucepan. Sweat the vegetables on a **very low heat**. After 15 minutes, the vegetables should be starting to collapse at the edges. Now add the stock, **replace the lid and simmer for about 20 minutes**, until the vegetables are **completely soft**.

2 Purée the soup in a liquidiser or with a hand-held
   blender. Taste and correct the seasoning and if
   the consistency is a little thick, thin it with some
   creamy milk or more stock.
3 Serve in hot bowls with a drizzle of herb oil and a
   scattering of toasted pumpkin seeds on each serving.

Herb Oil

4 tablespoons extra virgin olive oil

4 tablespoons chopped fresh herbs,
such as parsley, chives, marjoram,
sage and/or rosemary

1 fresh medium-hot red chilli,
deseeded and finely chopped

1 garlic clove, peeled and crushed to
a paste

zest of ¼ lemon

sea salt and freshly ground
black pepper

Use just one of the herbs or a combination of what is available to you. This oil is also delicious on simple grilled lamb, beef, pork or fish. **Makes 8 tablespoons**

Mix the oil, chopped herbs, chilli, garlic and lemon zest together and season with salt and pepper. Store in a jar in the fridge for up to a week.

Spiced Braised Leg of Lamb

2 tablespoons extra virgin olive oil

1 x 3.5kg leg of lamb, aitch
  bone removed

sea salt and freshly ground
  black pepper

425ml chicken stock (page 257)

2 tablespoons chopped fresh
  coriander

Spice mix

4 garlic cloves, peeled and
  finely chopped

1 dessertspoon chopped fresh
  rosemary

1 tablespoon fresh thyme leaves

3 teaspoons cumin seeds, left whole

2 teaspoons best-quality or
  homemade curry powder
  (page 258)

1½ teaspoons cumin seeds, lightly
  roasted and ground

1 teaspoon coriander seeds,
  left whole

½ teaspoon coriander seeds, lightly
  roasted and ground

To serve

mashed potatoes (page 190)

lemon wedges

fresh coriander leaves

This is an unusual recipe in that some of the spices are ground and some are left whole. Buy the best-quality curry powder or make your own (see my recipe on page 258) for even better results. Ask your butcher to remove the aitch bone from the leg of lamb, as this will make carving easier when the meat is cooked. **Serves 8–10**

1 Preheat the oven to 180°C.
2 Combine the garlic, herbs and spices in a bowl.
3 Heat the olive oil in a heavy-bottomed casserole set over a moderate heat and gently brown the meat on all sides, turning it several times to achieve an even result. If you don't have a casserole big enough to hold the leg of lamb, you can use a deep, heavy roasting tray instead. Browning the meat will take 10–15 minutes, so be patient with it, turning the meat to and fro as necessary. When the meat is browned, discard the oil and any fat that has rendered out of the lamb. Season the meat with salt and pepper and cover with the spice mixture. Some of it will fall off the lamb, but that's fine. Pour the stock into the casserole, avoiding the herb crust so that it doesn't get washed off the surface of the lamb.
4 Place a tight-fitting lid on the casserole, or if using a roasting tray, cover the lamb with a sheet of greaseproof paper and tightly seal the entire tray with foil. Transfer to the oven and cook for 1½ hours. When the lamb is cooked, remove it from the oven and reduce the temperature to 100°C. Place the meat on a serving dish and keep warm in the oven.
5 Degrease the cooking liquid by carefully spooning off any excess fat and return it to the saucepan. Discard the fat. Scrape about half of the spice mixture off the meat into the liquid. Simmer to

thicken the juices just slightly and to strengthen the flavour. Taste and correct the seasoning, then stir the chopped coriander into the gravy.

6 Carve the lamb into slices and serve with mashed potatoes, lemon wedges and a few whole coriander leaves and a sauceboat of gravy to pass around at the table.

Mashed Potatoes

900g floury potatoes, such as
Golden Wonder or Kerr's Pink,
unpeeled

sea salt and freshly ground
black pepper

approx. 120ml milk

50g butter

1 egg (optional)

Few dishes are more comforting than a bowl of mashed potatoes, but I know that some cooks are not always happy with their efforts. There are a few simple rules to follow for that bowl of perfectly smooth, fluffy mash. First, I buy local potatoes with the earth still on them rather than the prewashed ones, as I find the flavour to be far superior. Scrubbing them clean seems like a small sacrifice for the improved taste. Peel and mash the piping-hot potatoes as soon as they are cooked and always make sure that the milk you add is boiling. Keeping everything really hot is the key to fluffy, not sticky, mashed potatoes. Passing the hot, peeled, cooked potatoes through a vegetable mouli or potato ricer undoubtedly improves the texture, but an old-fashioned hand masher also works well. Use a floury variety of potato, such as a Golden Wonder or Kerr's Pink, and definitely don't try to make mashed potatoes with new potatoes, as they will be gluey and dull. **Serves 4**

1   Scrub the potatoes really well. Place in a saucepan, cover with cold water and salt generously. Cover the saucepan with a tight-fitting lid and bring to a boil, then turn the heat down to a simmer. The variety of potato and the time of year will determine how careful you will need to be when cooking the potatoes. The more floury the potatoes are, the more they are likely to split in the cooking, hence the more you need to steam them. In that case, pour off most of the water after about 10 minutes of cooking, just leaving 2cm of water to steam the potatoes for the remaining time, which takes about a further 20 minutes. The potatoes need to be completely tender.

2   **When the potatoes are nearly cooked, put the milk on to boil.** Immediately after the potatoes are cooked, peel them and pass through a vegetable mouli or potato ricer if you wish. This will give a

smoother consistency to the finished dish. If you don't have a mouli or ricer, use an old-fashioned hand masher. It is essential, however, to deal with the potatoes the minute they are cooked, as if they are allowed to cool at all before mashing, they may become gluey. **If your milk has gone off the boil, bring it back to a boil** and slowly add the boiling milk to the mashed potatoes. You may not need all the milk, so be careful not to make soup. Add the butter and egg (if using) and season well with salt and pepper. Mix well with a wooden spoon, taste and correct the seasoning. Serve hot.

Lime Oreos

140g butter, at room temperature

125g caster sugar

1 tablespoon sunflower oil

1 egg, beaten

1 teaspoon vanilla extract

225g plain flour

35g unsweetened cocoa powder

1 teaspoon baking powder

Buttercream filling

100g cold butter

150g icing sugar, sieved

zest and juice of 1 lime

To decorate

zest of 1 lime

This is my version of the beloved American cookie. The lime is terrific with the chocolate-flavoured biscuit and it helps to cut through the sweetness to achieve a good balance. Whether you are eating these in the time-honoured way with a glass of chilled milk or with the yogurt and banana ice that I suggest, they are good either way. **Makes 30 biscuits**

1 The biscuit dough can be made by hand or in a food mixer using the paddle attachment. Place the butter, sugar and oil in a large bowl. By hand with a wooden spoon or with the aid of a food mixer, cream together until light and fluffy in consistency and pale in colour. Add the egg and vanilla and beat again for one minute until well blended and smooth. Sieve the flour, cocoa and baking powder onto the mixture in the bowl and blend in gently but thoroughly until the mixture comes together into a dough and no longer looks streaky. **Do not over-mix.** Form the dough into a disc flattened to about 3cm thick, wrap in parchment paper and chill in the fridge for at least 30 minutes.

2 Preheat the oven to 180°C. Line two baking sheets with non-stick baking paper.

3 Working with half of the dough at a time, roll it out to about 5mm thick, using a little flour to prevent it from sticking (alternatively, roll it out between sheets of parchment paper). Cut out the biscuits with a 6cm cutter, then using a palette knife, place on the lined baking sheets. Leave a little space between the biscuits, as they swell slightly when cooking.

4 Bake in the oven for about 8 minutes. They will rise slightly and feel gently set to the touch. The biscuits crisp up as they cool. Place the baking sheets on a wire rack and allow the biscuits to cool, still on the paper.

5 Meanwhile, to make the buttercream, place the butter in a bowl and beat with a wooden spoon until pale in colour. Alternatively, you could use a food mixer fitted with the paddle attachment. Add the icing sugar, lime zest and juice and continue beating to a light and fluffy consistency.

6 Sandwich the cooled biscuits together with the buttercream, then finely grate the zest of the remaining lime all over the tops of the biscuits.

Yogurt and Banana Ice

500g organic full-fat natural yogurt

100g icing sugar

2 bananas

zest of 1 lime

This is so simple to make and is perfectly nice served on its own, but it pairs particularly well with the lime Oreos on page 193. **Serves 6**

1 Place the yogurt in a large bowl and sieve on the icing sugar. Peel and mash the bananas and add to the yogurt along with the lime zest. Give the mixture a quick purée with a hand-held blender to achieve a smooth consistency.

2 Freeze in an ice cream machine if you have one. Otherwise an excellent result is achieved by simply freezing it as it is. Store in the freezer and serve in neat scoops.

Winter

A vibrant salad with crisp textures is often a lovely start to a meal. It becomes easier to find good Irish dessert apples every year and they are at the centre of this salad. The Coolea cheese from County Cork pairs beautifully with the apple, hazelnuts and Brussels sprouts. The lack of the optional addition of the little-known myrtle berry should not put you off making this dish, but the shrub, *Myrtus ugni*, that produces these exquisite sweet berries late into the winter is perhaps the most trouble-free plant in my garden. They are as happy in a large pot as they are in the ground and I wouldn't be without them.

The palate-tickling salad tees the diner up for the robust flavours of beef, oysters and mushrooms. This dish can be prepared ahead of time, even a day or two before, but the addition of the oysters and mushrooms should be as close to the time of serving as possible. I feel this is a great celebration of land and sea and the best of what our island provides for us. A large bowl of mashed potatoes and an equally capacious bowl of a seasonal green vegetable such as kale or (more) Brussels sprouts are perfect alongside. It is worth noting that Brussels sprouts are often better earlier in the winter season than when traditionally eaten around Christmastime.

The richness of the beef is followed by a comforting but somewhat exotic rice pudding. The addition of coconut creates a perfect balance of the familiar and the perhaps unexpected. The simple cherry and orange compote is a great recipe, and in addition to serving it here with the rice, I also serve it with ice cream, meringues, on top of yogurt or with a wobbly junket. Some may feel that a rice pudding is not quite smart enough to finish a meal such as this, but when the rice is soft and warm and the compote and cream are both chilly, then in my opinion the overall effect of comfort, flavours that match and consistencies that enhance one another makes this dish smart enough to serve anywhere, anytime.

Salad of Apples, Coolea Cheese, Hazelnuts, Sprouts and Apple Syrup

25g unskinned hazelnuts

1 dessert apple, such as Cox's
  Orange Pippin, Irish Peach, Ard
  Cairn Russet or Egremont Russet

8 Brussels sprouts

8–12 radicchio leaves

8–12 sprigs of watercress

20 shavings of Coolea cheese

24–32 myrtle berries (optional)

sea salt and freshly ground black
  pepper

Dressing

juice of 1 lemon

4 tablespoons extra virgin olive oil

2 teaspoons apple syrup

In another meal this combination of ingredients could be served alongside grilled or roast pork. I search out Irish home-grown apples and I use an apple syrup from the marvellous Highbank Orchards in County Kilkenny. The Coolea cheese is from Macroom in County Cork and is another outstanding example of the quality of some of the artisan food being produced in Ireland now.

I have added myrtle berries as an optional ingredient here. If you don't have them growing, as most people will not, the salad is still great without them. However, the berries, which come from the Myrtus ugni *shrub, are really delicious – I use them in starters, main courses and desserts – and the evergreen plant is pretty much maintenance free and fruits year after year. It has small glossy leaves and produces sweet little red berries late in the year, when virtually all other fruit has disappeared for the winter. I highly recommend it as a beautiful thing to look at and a beautiful thing to eat.* **Serves 4**

1 Preheat the oven to 180°C.
2 Place the hazelnuts on a baking tray and roast in the oven for about 15 minutes, until the skins are starting to lift and flake and the nuts are golden brown. Remove the tray from the oven and allow the nuts to cool. Place the cold nuts in a clean kitchen towel, gather up the edges of the towel and rub the base of the towel on the palm of your hand to loosen the skins as much as possible. You will not get every last piece of skin off, but that's fine. Coarsely chop the nuts.
3 Whisk all the dressing ingredients together, taste and correct the seasoning. Store in a jar with a screw-top lid.
4 Cut the apple into quarters and remove the cores, then cut into slices 5mm thick. Remove the outer leaves of the sprouts and discard, then thinly slice the sprouts on a mandolin or by hand.

5 Combine the apples, sprouts, roasted hazelnuts, radicchio and watercress in a **large bowl**. Give the dressing a good shake and pour it over the ingredients. Use your hands to lightly lift and toss the salad.

6 Place the salad in a mound on a large wide serving dish. Scatter the Cooleea shavings over the salad and thread a few through the leaves as well. Add the myrtle berries now (if using). Sprinkle a small pinch of salt and pepper over the entire salad and serve as soon as possible.

Braised Beef with Rock Oysters and Oyster Mushrooms

1kg chuck of beef, trimmed of fat
and cut into 5cm cubes

3 tablespoons extra virgin olive oil

sea salt and freshly ground
black pepper

2 carrots, peeled and halved

1 white onion, peeled and halved

4 whole garlic cloves, unpeeled

150ml red wine

300ml homemade tomato purée
(page 259) or 2 tablespoons
tomato purée dissolved in
250ml water

150ml rich chicken or beef stock

1 bay leaf

1 branch of fresh thyme

12–16 rock oysters

20g butter

450g oyster mushrooms, small ones
left whole, larger ones sliced

2 tablespoons chopped fresh
flat-leaf or curly parsley

To serve
mashed potatoes (page 190)

This rich, robust stew pairs the flavours and textures of land and sea perfectly. The cut of beef here is crucial – to achieve a melting, unctuous result, I like to use the cut called chuck. This cut comes from the forequarters of the animal and needs long, slow cooking to tenderise the rather muscular flesh, but it yields a highly flavoured and delicious result. The silky oyster mushrooms are a good partner for the beef and the last-minute addition of the oysters and their juices makes for a deeply satisfying combination of ingredients. As the oysters are added to the pot just before it comes to the table so that they remain juicy and briny, you could reserve a little of the dish without the oysters for a guest who is not keen on them.

A rich buttery mashed potato is the perfect accompaniment, and if serving a green vegetable, which I normally would, then you have many possibilities. Slippery chard, garden or sea spinach, Brussels sprouts, any of the kales and any of the sprouting broccolis will all be lovely with the beef and the potatoes.

The braise can be made the day before, chilled overnight and reheated for the final addition of mushrooms and oysters on the day of serving. **Serves 6–8**

1 Preheat the oven to 150°C.

2 Heat a heavy-bottomed cast iron sauté pan on a moderate heat. **Dry the beef** lightly with kitchen paper. Add 1 tablespoon of the olive oil to the hot sauté pan and brown the meat on all sides in batches, seasoning the meat with salt and pepper as you go. **Don't overcrowd the meat in the pan** while browning or it will stew rather than develop a rich golden brown colour. Remove the coloured meat from the sauté pan, tip into a heavy-bottomed cast iron casserole and allow the sauté pan to heat up again before adding another tablespoon of oil and more meat. This stage is crucial for the depth of flavour in the finished dish.

3 When all the meat is sealed and coloured and has been removed from the sauté pan, add the carrots, onion and garlic and toss them in the pan for a moment or two to achieve a little colour, then add them to the meat in the casserole.

4 Now add the red wine to the sauté pan and allow to bubble and **reduce by half**. Gently scrape the bottom of the pan with a wooden spoon to loosen any caramelised meat juices into the liquid. Add the tomato purée, stock, bay leaf and thyme and bring to a simmer. Pour the liquid over the meat in the casserole and cover with a tight-fitting lid.

5 Place in the oven and cook for about 3 hours. I check the meat after 2½ hours and taste a little to see how tender it has become, but I usually find it takes the full 3 hours to achieve a meltingly succulent result.

6 When the meat is cooked, strain off all the cooking juices and allow to sit for a moment for the fat to rise to the surface. Remove the carrots, onions, thyme and bay from the casserole and discard, as they are not served in the finished dish. Strain the liquid through a maigret (a fat separator) to remove the fat or spoon it off. Taste the liquid – **if you are not happy with the flavour, place it in a wide pan, bring to a simmer and allow to reduce and concentrate for a few minutes**, until it tastes delicious. Add the juices back into the casserole with the meat.

7 Place the oysters in a tray and pop into the oven for 5 minutes or so. I use a bun tray and sit each oyster in it rounded side down, flat side up so as not to lose the precious oyster juices if they tumble over. Once you notice **liquid appearing on the tray**, it means the oysters are beginning to open and are ready. You are just firming up the oysters here, so don't leave them in the oven for too long or they will become overcooked, shrivelled and miserable. Remove the top shell, then carefully remove the oysters and their juices to a bowl.

8 Heat the remaining tablespoon of olive oil and the butter in a sauté pan and cook the mushrooms on a moderate heat for about 5 minutes, until coloured and wilted. Season with salt and pepper and add to the casserole. Bring the casserole back to a simmer and taste and correct the seasoning.

9 Slip the oysters and their juices in on top of the meat. Scatter on the chopped parsley, ladle the stew into warmed bowls and serve with creamy mashed potatoes.

Coconut Rice Pudding with Sour Cherry and Orange Compote

100g Arborio rice

50g desiccated coconut

50g caster sugar

10g butter

1.2 litres milk

1 teaspoon vanilla extract

To serve

sour cherry and orange compote
   (page 208)

chilled softly whipped cream

I love this combination of flavours, which elevates the humble rice pudding to a higher plane. The compote is best cooked well in advance to allow the cherries to swell and soften and the juices to become syrupy and somewhat concentrated. I usually cook the cherries the day before, but cooked first thing in the morning to serve that evening, they will also yield a good result. The pudding is best served warm with chilled softly whipped cream to accompany. The preparation time here is short, but do give the rice the suggested length of time to cook to a creamy consistency. **Serves 6–8**

1 Preheat the oven to 180°C.
2 Put the rice, coconut, sugar and butter into a 2 litre capacity pie dish. Bring the milk to the boil with the vanilla and pour it over the rice. Give everything a gentle stir.
3 Bake in the oven for 1½–2 hours and remove when just set. The skin on the pudding should be golden and the rice underneath should be cooked through and have soaked up the milk, but **it should still be soft and creamy**.
4 Serve the pudding warm with the cherry compote chilled or at room temperature and chilled softly whipped cream on the side.

Sour Cherry and Orange Compote

100g dried sour cherries

40g caster sugar

250ml orange juice

This is a simple and lovely thing that has a myriad of uses. It is perfect served with the warm rice pudding on page 206, but it is also great with vanilla ice cream or indeed caramel or coffee. I drizzle it over meringues or over a bowl of yogurt or porridge. It is delicious with either hot or cold chocolate desserts and would be terrific with the chocolate soufflé cake on page 96 or the chocolate and caramel whip on page 165. **Serves 6–8**

Place all the ingredients for the compote in a small saucepan. **Bring to a simmer and cook gently for 5 minutes.** Remove from the heat and allow to cool, then cover and leave to macerate overnight. As the compote cools, the juices thicken slightly to a light syrupy consistency.

Beef and oysters are a classic combination, but perhaps not as expected in this starter. The thinly flattened raw beef and briny mayonnaise with punchy wild greens are a terrific and savoury start to the meal. I like to serve thinly sliced brown bread and butter on the side. Even though I have placed this firmly in winter, as I find rock oysters more delicious to eat during the cooler months of the year, it could also be very good in spring and autumn.

Ham hocks are a favourite of mine, with a wonderful flavour coming from the skin and bone. The texture is best if you cook them to the point where the meat is still attached to the bone, but only just – a gentle push of a fork is all it should take for the juicy ham to slide away. The ridiculously easy sauce is perfect and I don't know how it took me so long to come up with this idea. The hocks are really good value for money and any leftover meat makes a perfect sandwich filling. They are also terrific served with the shaved cauliflower salad on page 249.

The combination of vanilla mousse and espresso jelly for dessert here is smooth and smart. The shiny, strong coffee jelly is a good foil for the delicate vanilla-flecked cream. A glass serving dish is definitely best for the presentation of this dish, as the appearance of the floating dark jelly is rather dramatic. The entire dish can be made in advance and will sit happily in the fridge once tightly covered for a couple of days.

Beef Carpaccio with Oyster Mayonnaise and Wild Greens

200g fillet of beef, trimmed of all fat and grizzle

4 teaspoons extra virgin olive oil, plus extra to serve

sea salt and freshly ground black pepper

4 tablespoons oyster mayonnaise (page 213)

20 sprigs of wild greens or small rocket leaves

4 winter radishes, thinly sliced (optional)

Beef and oysters are two ingredients we have in quality and abundance in Ireland, so it is a pity that they are not seen together on more menus, as they are a great combination. I have also paired the duo in the braised beef recipe on page 202, but the treatment here is very different. Raw beef is not to everybody's taste, but it can be utterly delicious when the beef is of beautiful quality and it is also a great way to make a small piece of expensive beef stretch to many servings. The oyster mayonnaise is easy and can be made a few hours ahead of time and chilled, as can the beef, so all in all, this is a dish you can be very organised with.

When serving the beef, I use whatever seasonal wild greens I can find that will complement the beef and oysters, such as watercress, bittercress, chickweed, wild sorrel, wood sorrel or pennywort. If you can't find wild greens, some small rocket leaves would work very nicely. Occasionally I will have a few radishes that will be surviving the cold weather and I will slice those on thinly for a peppery kick. If eating raw beef is out of the question for you, try the oyster mayonnaise with a thin slice of sirloin or fillet of beef grilled until rare. **Serves 4**

1 Cut the beef into four even slices. Dab each piece of beef, top and bottom, with a teaspoon of olive oil. The purpose of the oil is to flavour the beef and to help it to spread.

2 Place a sheet of parchment paper on your worktop and put a piece of beef on the lower half of the paper. Fold over the upper portion of the paper to cover the beef. The piece of beef should be sitting in the middle of the paper so that it has room to spread in all directions. Take a rolling pin and start gently rolling over the paper and the beef. The beef will stretch and spread. Roll it until it has almost **trebled in size**. **Chill** the rolled beef in its paper sheet and roll the other pieces of beef in the same way.

3 To serve, unwrap each piece of beef onto a plate. I do this by lifting back the top piece of paper and quickly inverting the beef onto the plate, then gently peeling off the rest of the paper. Season each piece of beef with a few grains of sea salt and black pepper. Drizzle a little oyster mayonnaise over the beef and scatter on the greens and radishes (if using). Finish each serving with a few drops of olive oil and serve.

Oyster Mayonnaise

1 egg yolk

1 tablespoon lemon juice

pinch of dry English mustard powder

100ml sunflower oil

4 rock oysters and their juices

sea salt and freshly ground
   black pepper

This simple sauce is perfect with the raw beef carpaccio on page 210. It would also be terrific with a grilled fillet or sirloin steak with some pickled red onions (page 105) on the side. I use the milder sunflower oil in this mayonnaise recipe, as olive oil, which is more pronounced in flavour, can overpower the subtlety of the oysters. **Serves 4**

Place the egg yolk, lemon juice and mustard in the bowl of a small food processor. Switch on the machine and dribble the sunflower oil through the feeder tube in a **slow but steady drizzle**. The sauce will begin to emulsify and thicken. When all the oil has been added, add the oysters and enough of their juices to achieve the consistency of thick pouring cream after pulsing briefly. Taste and correct the seasoning. **Chill the mayonnaise until serving.** This sauce is best eaten on the day that it is made. If I have any left over, I discard it.

Ham Hocks with Mustard and Chive Cream

4 fresh ham hocks

2 celery sticks, chopped

1 onion, peeled and halved

1 carrot, thickly sliced

4 garlic cloves, unpeeled

1 bay leaf

6 black peppercorns

To serve

mustard and chive cream
(page 215)

celery with tomatoes, fennel and
raisins (page 217)

I love ham hocks and they are very easy to cook. They are tremendously good value and are delicious served hot, warm or at room temperature. I prefer then unsmoked, but that is a personal choice. The leftover cooking water makes a delicious stock for soups, so don't discard it. **Serves 4**

1 Place all the ingredients into a large saucepan and cover with cold water. Bring to the boil, then reduce the heat and simmer, covered, for 2–2½ hours or even longer, until the meat is almost falling off the bone.

2 Serve with the mustard and chive cream on the side and the celery with tomatoes, fennel and raisins.

Mustard and Chive Cream

1 teaspoon dry Colman's English
   mustard powder
1 teaspoon hot water
120ml softly whipped cream
1 tablespoon finely chopped
   fresh chives
sea salt and freshly ground
   black pepper

This could not be easier to make, but I feel that the dry Colman's English mustard powder is essential for a fiery yet comforting accompaniment to the ham on page 214. This sauce is also delicious served with roast beef. **Serves 4**

Blend the dry mustard and hot water to form a wet paste. Fold it through the softly whipped cream along with the chives and a pinch of salt and pepper. Keep chilled until serving.

Celery with Tomatoes, Fennel and Raisins

3 tablespoons extra virgin olive oil

500g celery, sliced at an angle into pieces 1cm thick

100g onion, peeled and thinly sliced

1 large garlic clove, peeled and crushed to a paste

1 branch of fresh thyme

2 teaspoons roasted and ground fennel seeds

sea salt and freshly ground black pepper

450g ripe tomatoes, peeled and chopped, or 1 x 400g tin of good-quality tinned chopped tomatoes

2 tablespoons raisins

1 teaspoon red wine vinegar

2 tablespoons coarsely chopped celery leaves (optional)

Celery has somewhat gone out of fashion, which is a shame as it is a very flavoursome vegetable. I like it either raw and crisp, or cooked and tender. Anything in between seems unsatisfactory. I suppose you could call this dish a vegetable stew – it can be cooked in advance and reheats perfectly at a later stage. I serve this with boiled ham or bacon, roast or grilled pork or with venison. The addition of the raisins enlivens and slightly sweetens the dish. If some celery leaves come with the head of celery, I chop those coarsely and sprinkle them over the dish just before it goes to the table.
Serves 6–8

1 Heat the olive oil in a heavy-bottomed saucepan set over a moderate heat. Add the celery, onion, garlic, thyme and fennel seeds. Toss everything in the oil, season with salt and pepper and cover the pan with a tight-fitting lid. Reduce the heat to low and cook on a very gentle heat to sweat and tenderise the vegetables. **It is crucial that the celery and onions are tender before adding the tomatoes.** This should take about 15 minutes.

2 Gently mix in the tomatoes, raisins and vinegar and season with salt and pepper. **Cover** and cook at a gentle simmer for about 10 minutes, until the tomatoes have collapsed to form a sauce. Taste and correct the seasoning. The dish can be served now or reheated later. Scatter over the celery leaves (if using) just before serving.

St Tola Goat's Cheese with PX Raisins, *p240*

Orange and Passion Fruit
Granita with Mango, Banana
and Lime, *p252*

Salad of Shaved Cauliflower
and Brussels Sprouts
with Red Onions, Raisin
and Parmesan, *p249*

Spiced Beef, *p246*

Vanilla Mousse with Espresso Jelly

600ml cream

50g caster sugar

1 vanilla pod, split in half lengthways

2 teaspoons powdered gelatine

3 tablespoons cold water

Espresso jelly

1¼ teaspoons powdered gelatine

2 tablespoons cold water

45g caster sugar

approx. 200ml very strong hot
    filter coffee

This is a delicious variation on a classic panna cotta. The combination came about when I collaborated with JR Ryall, the pastry chef at Ballymaloe House, for a dinner that we work on every autumn. The entire dessert can be made a day in advance and chilled and will keep happily for a few days, although the sooner you eat it, the more delicious it will be. We served the mousse in a tall glass pedestal bowl and it looked wonderful, but you can of course use whatever dish you really like. Serve with langues de chat biscuits (page 168) for a special treat. If I am serving this dish in summer or autumn, I often accompany it with a bowl of fresh raspberries. **Serves 6–8**

1 Put the cream in a heavy-bottomed saucepan with the sugar and split vanilla pod. Put the pan on a low heat and **bring to the shivery stage**.

2 Meanwhile, sponge the gelatine in the cold water for a few minutes in a Pyrex or pottery bowl. I prefer not to use plastic or stainless steel here, as the gelatine can overheat more easily and stick to those lighter, thinner surfaces. The gelatine will take on a sponge-like appearance.

3 Place the bowl of sponged gelatine into a saucepan of **barely simmering water** and allow to dissolve until it looks completely clear. There is no need to stir it at this stage. As soon as the mixture is clear, **add the warm cream to the gelatine**, stirring all the time.

4 Now strain the cream mixture through a fine sieve to remove the vanilla pod. If necessary, squeeze the pod to extract more vanilla seeds into the cream. Allow the cream to cool to room temperature before pouring into your serving dish or dishes. To save time, the hot cream can be stirred over an ice bath to cool it down faster. Allowing the cream to cool before decanting it into the serving dish will prevent the vanilla seeds from pooling in

the bottom of the bowl. Instead, they will stay in suspension and look much prettier, especially if you are serving the mousse in a glass bowl.

5 Place in the fridge and allow to set fully. This will take at least 2 hours.

6 While the cream is setting, make the espresso jelly. Sponge the gelatine in the water and dissolve as above in gently simmering water until clear.

7 Place the sugar in a measuring jug and add enough hot coffee until there is exactly 200ml in total. Stir to dissolve the sugar, then add the sweetened coffee to the gelatine, stirring all the time.

8 **Allow the coffee to cool completely but remain liquid.** Again, you can speed this up by placing the bowl of coffee in an ice bath. Carefully spoon the cooled – but not yet set – coffee jelly onto the set vanilla mousse. Return to the fridge and allow to set fully, which will take about 3 hours.

If you look at cauliflower closely, it is an extraordinary-looking vegetable: a great big flower at its centre surrounded by a large frill of leaves. My only issue with cauliflower is that you only ever get a few of the green leaves, which I like as much as the flower itself. It seems such a shame that all that edible greenery is thrown away. Whenever the opportunity arises to get a cauliflower with the green leaves still attached, I grab it with both hands. In any event, this is a simple way to cook cauliflower in the modern fashion and a long way away from a gratin of cauliflower cheese, which is of course still a really lovely dish. We have only recently realised in this part of the world that this vegetable will happily lap up Indian, South-East Asian, Mediterranean, Mexican, North African and Middle Eastern seasoning and spicing with aplomb. In this recipe cumin adds a little exotic lift and the caramelised onions add depth. I am combining it with a Syrian sauce, muhammara, and I think they work really well together. Don't forget, though, that this simple cauliflower dish can be served on its own as a vegetable to accompany roast or grilled meat and poultry. The muhammara recipe is equally useful in its own right to serve with roast or grilled meat, poultry or oily fish such as mackerel, salmon or mullet.

Sweet-tasting celeriac is the basis for the main course of crisp fried fritters. The combination of that sweetness with the pear is very good, and when tempered by the sharpness of the bitter radicchio and capers, it make an excellent savoury combination. When frying in oil, do be very careful to keep your oil at the correct temperature. If the oil is too cool, the food being fried will soak up the fat and be heavy and greasy. On the other hand, if the oil is too hot, the food will colour too quickly and not be cooked through. If I am not using a deep fat fryer, I use a probe thermometer to check the temperature of the oil. The small dollop of mayonnaise that I serve with the fritters may sound superfluous, but I find it to be the perfect sauce that adds a little richness, but not too much.

I love the warm winter pudding to end this meal. Apples, chocolate and mincemeat are a real hit together, though if you are being true to the meat-free theme of this meal, then make sure your mincemeat is vegetarian. This is not a glamorous pudding, it is a comfort pudding, but I make no apologies for its lack of visual style. Comfort food is sometimes needed to be just what it suggests – unchallenging and full of heart-warming deliciousness.

Roasted Cauliflower with Red Onion, Cumin and Muhammara

1 head of cauliflower, green
   leaves removed

1 large red onion, peeled and
   thinly sliced

3 teaspoons cumin seeds, roasted
   and ground

zest of 1 lemon

sea salt and freshly ground
   black pepper

6 tablespoons extra virgin olive oil

1 batch of muhammara (page 226)

6–7 walnuts, roasted and coarsely
   chopped

½ pomegranate, seeds removed

2 tablespoons stoned and coarsely
   chopped green olives

2 tablespoons chopped fresh
   coriander leaves

The preparation for this dish can be done several hours in advance, though I prefer not to cook it until closer to the time of serving. The vegetable is good served straight from the oven or at room temperature. The cauliflower in this recipe can be replaced with the exotic-looking green cauliflower called Romanesco.

The muhammara I suggest to serve with the cauliflower in this meal is spread over the base of your serving dishes and then the cauliflower is neatly piled on top. Finish the dish with the green olives, walnuts, pomegranate seeds and coriander leaves sprinkled over the roasted cauliflower.

Don't forget to serve the roasted cauliflower in another meal without the muhammara as a standalone vegetable.
Serves 6–8

1 Preheat the oven to 200°C.

2 Separate the cauliflower into florets and place in a large bowl. If the leaves are in good shape, roughly chop them and their stalks and add them too. Add the onion, ground cumin, lemon zest, salt and pepper and enough olive oil to glaze the vegetables.

3 Place on a roasting tray and roast in the oven for about 30 minutes, turning the vegetables once or twice during the cooking time. The cauliflower and onion should be well coloured and tender. Don't worry if the onion gets quite caramelised, as this will just add to the flavour.

4 To serve, spread the muhammara over the base of your serving dish or individual plates. Make neat piles of cauliflower on top, leaving some of the deeply coloured sauce visible around the bottom of the cauliflower. Finish the dish with the walnuts, pomegranate seeds, green olives and coriander.

Muhammara

1 red pepper, deseeded and cut into
 large chunks

1 large red onion, peeled and cut
 into 6 wedges

8 cherry tomatoes

1–2 fresh red chillies, stalks removed
 and deseeded if very hot

6 garlic cloves, unpeeled

2 tablespoons extra virgin olive oil

sea salt and freshly ground
 black pepper

70g walnuts, roughly chopped

2 tablespoons pomegranate
 molasses

1 teaspoon smoked paprika

½ teaspoon roasted and ground
 cumin seeds

I find this flavour-packed Syrian sauce to be really useful. When you have a jar of this in the fridge, you will never be stuck for a sauce to serve with roast and grilled meat, poultry or oily fish. It makes a quick snack smeared onto grilled bread (page 16) or hot toast and I love it with a hard-boiled egg. Be brave when roasting the vegetables to achieve plenty of colour, as that is where the depth of flavour in the recipe comes from. I once omitted the walnuts when I made this sauce for a friend who could not eat them and it was still good, though different.
Serves 4

1 Preheat the oven to 220°C.
2 Place the pepper, onion, tomatoes, chilli and garlic on a roasting tray, drizzle with 1 tablespoon of the olive oil and season with salt and pepper. Roast in the oven for 20–25 minutes, until the vegetables are starting to char slightly.
3 Meanwhile, place the walnuts on a hot dry sauté pan set over a medium heat and cook, stirring often, until they are nicely toasted.
4 When the vegetables are roasted, squeeze the roasted garlic cloves out of their skins and place in a food processor along with the roasted vegetables. Add the toasted walnuts, the remaining tablespoon of olive oil, pomegranate molasses, smoked paprika and cumin and pulse until you have achieved a textured dip. Taste and correct the seasoning.

Celeriac Fritters with Pears, Walnuts, Radicchio and Caper Mayonnaise

sunflower oil, for deep frying

120g celeriac (weight after peeling), peeled and cut into fine julienne, like long matchsticks

12 watercress sprigs

12 radicchio leaves

1 ripe pear, cut in quarters lengthways, cored and thinly sliced

16 walnut halves

4 generous teaspoons homemade mayonnaise (page 258)

28 capers

Batter

140g plain flour

pinch of salt

1½ tablespoons extra virgin olive oil

100ml water

1 large egg white, beaten until quite stiff

Dressing

6 tablespoons extra virgin olive oil

2 tablespoons lemon juice

½ teaspoon honey

sea salt and freshly ground black pepper

Celeriac, or root celery, as it is sometimes called, is a terrific vegetable. It make a marvellous soup, is great roasted or as a purée and is the essential ingredient in the classic remoulade, in which case it is eaten raw. The flavour of celeriac is milder and sweeter than the green celery we are more familiar with.

These crisp fritters are served here as a main course but would also be very good as a starter, in which case the recipe would serve eight people. I use peppery watercress sprigs and radicchio leaves here, but you could substitute a mixture of leaves. **Makes 4**

1 Make the batter for frying the fritters first. Place the flour and a pinch of salt in a large bowl. Add the olive oil and whisk in enough water to form a smooth batter the consistency of thick cream. Chill for 30 minutes, then fold in the stiffly beaten egg white.

2 Whisk all the dressing ingredients together. Taste and correct the seasoning.

3 When ready to cook the fritters, heat 10cm of sunflower oil in a heavy-bottomed cast iron or stainless steel saucepan until it reaches 180°C, or if you have a deep fat fryer, that will work perfectly.

4 Mix the celeriac through the batter. Gently drop four large spoonfuls of the mixture into the hot oil and cook until crisp and golden brown on both sides, which should take about 10 minutes in total. Remove from the oil, drain on kitchen paper and keep warm in a low oven. They will remain crisp for 20 minutes or so.

5 To serve, place the salad leaves, sliced pear and walnuts in a large bowl and dress with the well-mixed dressing. Divide between four plates and place a fritter on top of each salad. Drop 1 teaspoon of mayonnaise on top of the fritters and scatter on the capers. Add a few grains of sea salt and serve immediately.

Winter Chocolate Apple Pudding

1kg Bramley apples, peeled, cored
   and cut into large chunks
30g butter
2 tablespoons water

For the crumb layer
150g mincemeat
125g soft white breadcrumbs
75g light soft brown sugar
50g dark chocolate (at least 70%
   cocoa solids), roughly chopped
75g butter
3 tablespoons golden syrup

To serve
chilled softly whipped cream

*This is a variation of the classic apple betty, which is a simple pudding that I love. This combination of bitter cooking apple, chocolate and the flavours of Christmas mincemeat is also charming. This is an ideal vehicle for using up last year's mincemeat. The pudding needs to be served warm on hot plates with cold softly whipped cream on the side. **Serves 4***

1 Preheat the oven to 190°C.
2 Put the apples in a pan and toss with the butter and water over a gentle heat. Cook for about 10 minutes, until the apples start to soften and are collapsing just a little at the edges but still generally keeping their shape. Tip them into a 1.5-litre baking dish.
3 Mix together the mincemeat, breadcrumbs, sugar and chocolate and cover the apples loosely with this topping. Melt the butter and golden syrup together in a small saucepan and pour it over the crumbs, making certain to soak them all.
4 Bake in the oven for 35 minutes, until the apple is soft and the crumbs are golden and crisp. Allow to cool slightly, then serve in heated bowls with chilled softly whipped cream.

It seems that kale has taken over the world in the last few years in terms of being the winter vegetable of choice, but one wonders if we have peaked in our fascination with what for so long was seen as a dull and torturous green. The peaks and troughs of the curly leaf are a prime example of fashion in food and the way ingredients rise and fall in popularity as their supposed miraculous properties are going to have all of us jumping out of our skins. I have always had a happy relationship with kale, and though not as hysterical as some of its supporters, I suspect I will still be loyal to it even when the next 'wonder food' is announced and the food fashion victims have galloped on to the next life-changing leaf. A fresh, cleanly grown food of almost any description will be good for you as long as it is part of a varied and balanced diet. No single food will lead to a happy and healthy life. Speaking of happiness, this soup, where the kale is combined with earthy, healthy lentils, certainly makes me feel great. I suggest that the soup be served with quite a thick consistency, though of course you can serve it just as you like it at your table. The quality of the olive oil that is the final addition is really important, and the better the oil is, the more exciting the eating of the soup will be.

Winter brings other leaves, and the bitter red radicchio and peppery watercress are favourites. When combined with sweet oranges, which are also at their best now, and a few slices of juicy grilled duck, it is a winning combination. I have allowed two duck breasts to feed four people in this recipe, as I think that with the leaves, orange segments and the accompanying cake of matchstick potatoes, it is a good balance that will satisfy but not steamroll.

The final course in this meal is a combination of savoury goats' cheese with sweet sherry-soaked raisins. The flavours work really well together, and even though the presentation is relatively simple, it still looks lovely. The sweet raisins have many other uses and will keep in the fridge for months, so don't discard them if you have some left over. I also serve them with chicken livers, ice creams, blue cheese and chocolate desserts. I think this dish is a good example of how simple it can be sometimes to bring something utterly delicious to the table.

Lentil and Kale Soup

250g dried green lentils

1 onion, peeled and halved

3 garlic cloves, unpeeled

1 fresh red chilli, left whole

1 bay leaf

1 branch of fresh thyme

1–1.2 litres chicken stock (page 257)

sea salt and freshly ground
    black pepper

500g curly kale (weight after the
    tough stalks have been removed)

150ml cream

best-quality extra virgin olive oil,
    for drizzling

This is a nourishing combination of ingredients that makes a soup that is deeply satisfying to eat. I serve this soup with a very thick consistency in the Italian style. If you prefer the soup thinner, though, just add more stock to the lentils when cooking. A drizzle of the very best olive oil is the perfect finishing touch and that last-minute addition seems to elevate this rustic soup to a much more sophisticated plateau.
Serves 6–8

1 Place the lentils, onion, garlic, chilli, bay leaf, thyme and chicken stock in a saucepan and bring to a simmer. Cover and cook very gently until the lentils are tender, which should take about 20 minutes, though that will vary depending on the age, size and variety of the lentils being used. Don't allow the lentils to become overcooked and mushy, but at the same time they do need to be completely cooked all the way through. I add a good pinch of salt to the lentils 5 minutes before they are cooked.

2 Remove the onion, bay leaf and thyme and discard. Peel the skin off the chilli and discard it, then split the chilli in half lengthways and remove and discard the seeds. Chop the chilli flesh finely and add it back into the lentils. Press the flesh out of the cooked garlic and discard the skins, then stir the soft garlic into the lentils. Taste and correct the seasoning.

3 Bring 3 litres of water to a boil in a large saucepan and season well with salt. Add the kale leaves and cook, uncovered, for about 8 minutes, until completely tender. Strain off all the water and place the leaves in a food processor. Pulse briefly, then add the cream and purée to a smooth consistency. Taste and correct the seasoning, making sure to add some freshly ground black pepper. Both elements of the soup can be put aside now for reheating later.

4 When ready to serve the soup, reheat the lentils and kale in separate saucepans. When both mixtures are simmering, add the kale to the lentil saucepan and gently fold it through. The soup can look streaky at this stage, but that is the way I prefer to serve it. Ladle into hot soup bowls and drizzle each serving with your best extra virgin olive oil. Serve immediately.

Grilled Duck Breast with a Salad of Oranges, Watercress and Radicchio

2 oranges

pinch of caster sugar

3 tablespoons extra virgin olive oil

1 tablespoon lemon juice

sea salt and freshly ground black
  pepper

2 large duck breasts

2 handfuls of watercress, washed
  and dried

2 handfuls of radicchio leaves,
  washed and dried

To serve:

pommes allumettes (page 238)
  or rustic roast potatoes with
  balsamic butter (page 107)

*Duck and oranges are a classic combination of flavours, but here the emphasis is on a lighter result rather than the rich sauce one normally expects. Peppery watercress and bitter red-leaved radicchio are a lively foil for the richness of the meat. A selection of salad leaves could replace the ones I have suggested, but including some bitter leaves makes all the difference to the balance of the finished dish. The vinaigrette used to dress the salad leaves also becomes the sauce, so the overall effect is somewhat refreshing. I like to serve a crisp potato dish to accompany, such as a pommes allumettes or rustic roast potatoes. I think two large duck breasts, when being served with accompanying vegetables and potatoes, are sufficient for four people, but you will know what is needed at your table. **Serves 2–4***

1 Preheat the oven to 100°C.
2 Zest one of the oranges with a Microplane or on a fine grater. Carefully segment both oranges and sprinkle with a pinch of sugar. Mix the orange zest with the olive oil, lemon juice and salt and pepper to make the vinaigrette. Taste and correct the seasoning. Add the oranges to the vinaigrette and give them a gentle stir.
3 **Place a cold grill pan on a medium heat and immediately put the duck breasts on the cold pan, skin side down.** This seems like such an odd thing to do and contradicts most of the normal rules of grilling meat, but it works quite brilliantly, as while the skin is slowly crisping, the liquid fat renders out of the duck. Save all that duck fat for roasting potatoes and vegetables – it will keep covered in the fridge for months. Cook the duck on that medium heat until the skin has become crispy and a rich deep golden colour. This takes about 10 minutes. Turn over and finish cooking the duck on the other side for about 7 minutes more. By now

the centres of the breasts should be pink, which is the way I like to serve them. I don't like duck served rare as I find it to be tough. Rest the cooked duck breasts in the low oven for at least 5 minutes but up to 30 minutes – the juices will be more evenly distributed through the flesh after resting. I put a **small plate upside down sitting on top of a bigger plate** and sit the breasts against the sloping edges of the upside-down plate. This way, any juices that run out of the duck breasts will be saved, and equally importantly, the meat will not be stewing in its own juices.

4 When ready to serve, assemble the ingredients on a large hot serving dish or individual plates. Toss the leaves in just enough of the well-mixed vinaigrette to make them glisten, then divide between the hot plates. Carve the duck breasts into neat slices and scatter through the leaves. Arrange the orange segments through the salad leaves and duck slices and drizzle on the remaining vinaigrette. **I like to quickly reheat any of the cooking juices from the resting duck and add those as a final lick of flavour.** Serve immediately with the pommes allumettes or rustic roast potatoes on the side.

Pommes Allumettes

50g butter, at room temperature

8–10 large Golden Wonder
    potatoes, peeled and cut into long
    matchsticks

sea salt and freshly ground
    black pepper

*Don't be put off by the prospect of having to cut all the potatoes into matchstick-sized pieces. If you have someone to help, it adds to the fun and halves the job. This cake is good with all roast and grilled meats and with grilled fish. Cook the cake on a gentle heat with a tight-fitting lid to keep the steam in the pan – I like to use a heavy-bottomed cast iron pan. Just be careful when turning the cake out onto a hot serving dish. I sometimes use this recipe as a vehicle for leftover scraps of roast chicken, lamb or ham. Just scatter the little pieces of cooked meat through the potatoes when assembling the dish and you will end up with a satisfying lunch or supper dish that only needs a mixed leaf salad (page 49) or a green vegetable to make a terrifically good family meal. **Serves 8–10***

1 Rub the base and sides of a 22cm pan generously with about half of the butter. If your pan is a little bigger or smaller, just adjust the quantity of potato accordingly. Press the potatoes into the pan and season well with salt and pepper. Dot the remaining butter over the surface of the potatoes. Cover the potatoes with greaseproof paper, then cover the pan with a **tight-fitting lid**. Place on a **very low heat** and cook for approximately 25 minutes. Remove the lid and check that the potatoes are very tender and cooked through. If not, replace the paper and lid and cook for a further 5–10 minutes.

2 When cooked, remove the paper and lid from the pan and place a hot serving dish, serving side down, on top of the pan. **Using a dry cloth to protect your hands from the heat of the pan, carefully flip over the potatoes onto the plate.** Remove the pan. The top of the potato cake should be golden and crispy. Serve immediately or keep hot in a moderate oven (180°C).

St Tola Goats' Cheese with PX Raisins

30g raisins

2 tablespoons Pedro Ximénez
(PX) sherry

4 slices of St Tola goats' cheese ash
log (approx. 100g)

16–20 small rocket leaves

2 tablespoons extra virgin olive oil

squeeze of lemon juice

sea salt and freshly cracked
black pepper

Good shopping is crucial if you are to put delicious food on the table, and this dish perfectly illustrates how thoughtful shopping for just a few ingredients can yield the most delicious and sophisticated results with virtually no cooking involved. We are so lucky in Ireland that over the last 20 years, a whole raft of committed food producers have been creating products that help us to achieve our daily goal of great-tasting and health-giving food. St Tola goats' cheese made in County Clare is a shining and outstanding example of the quality of the world-class foods that we can now buy, take home, simply unwrap and eat.

In this very simple recipe, which I serve in this instance to finish this meal, the addition of the sweet sherry-soaked raisins gets over the problem of no dessert being served and they are terrific with the pleasantly salty cheese. I like to use the ash-covered log from St Tola for this dish. In another meal this dish would be perfect served as a starter.

The sherry I use here, Pedro Ximénez San Emilio sherry from Jerez in Spain, is super-sweet with a real depth of flavour and is a great aid to any cook. It also pairs brilliantly with blue cheese, chocolate desserts or chicken livers, either pan fried or in a pâté, and is a great drizzle for a vanilla, coffee or caramel ice cream.

Serve a crisp cracker or hot and crispy white bread with this dish. **Serves 4**

1 Place the raisins in a small saucepan and pour over the sherry. Bring to a simmer and cook for 5 minutes. Transfer to a small container and **leave to soak for 6 hours or overnight**. The raisins will soak up some of the sherry and the remaining sherry will become syrupy.

2 Place a slice of cheese on each serving plate. Scatter the rocket leaves around the cheese, making sure that the beautiful black line of ash on the outside of the cheese is visible in its entirety. Drizzle the

olive oil over the leaves and a little over the cheese, then squeeze a little lemon juice to follow the olive oil. Carefully divide the sherry-soaked raisins and syrupy juices between the plates and finish each serving with a small twist of black pepper and a few grains of sea salt.

The parsnip soup in this meal is warm and
comforting with a silky-smooth consistency – exactly
what is needed in the colder months of the year.
The deeply flavoured and richly coloured harissa
brings a more sophisticated air to this underrated
vegetable and looks beautiful floating on top of the
pale-coloured soup. The recipe can also be treated
like a master recipe for other winter vegetables, as the
parsnips I am using here can be replaced with carrots,
swede turnips or leeks, all of which will sit happily
with the harissa. A recipe like this, where you can vary
the ingredients somewhat to reflect what is in season
and in good condition, is a really useful tool for all
cooks.

Spiced beef is such an essential part of winter and
Christmas for many people and I have come to love it
even though it was not really something I ate growing
up. Nowadays I could not imagine not having it to eat
at least once during the festive period. I have added
some cinnamon and star anise to the spicing of the
beef here and I feel it brings a fresh lightness to the
flavours. The beef needs to marinate in the spices for
up to a week, but all you do during that period is give
it a little turn in its container once a day. I slice the
cooked beef very thinly, as you don't need to serve too
much since the flavour is so intense.

The shaved cauliflower salad is a perfect accompaniment to the beef and it looks really pretty if you
add the pomegranate seeds. The overall effect of
the somewhat creamy consistency of the dressing
surrounding the crisp raw vegetables is deliciously
savoury. After a week or so of eating the traditional
foods that we love at Christmas, this should come as a
refreshing change.

Speaking of change, the granita and accompanying
fruit, which sings of warm, exotic and faraway places,
is also the sort of flavour I yearn for at the end of the
year. Days are at their shortest, nights are at their
longest and I need something to remind me that the
sun will return, the sky will be blue and we will dip
our toes in warm sea water again. At this time of year
I sometimes need the ingredients from another part
of the world that shriek of summer. This granita is a
delicious taste of palm-fringed beaches and a bright
and optimistic way to end a winter meal.

Parsnip Soup with Harissa

25g butter

1 tablespoon extra virgin olive oil

500g parsnips, peeled and diced

100g potato, peeled and diced

100g white onion, peeled and diced

1 garlic clove, peeled and sliced

sea salt and freshly ground
  black pepper

750ml chicken stock (page 257)

splash of cream (optional)

2 tablespoons harissa (page 264)

best-quality extra virgin olive oil,
  for drizzling

Winter root vegetables like the parsnip are terrific value for money and packed full of flavour. They seem to yield the deep, comforting taste we long for at this time of year. I always buy my root vegetables unwashed – in other words, with some of the soil they grew in still attached. They have a great deal more flavour than ones that have had their protective coat of earth scrubbed off and also keep much better and for longer than the cleaned ones. It is of course a little more work for you at home, but the difference in flavour and texture is enormous – quite simply, there is no comparison. **Serves 6–8**

1 Melt the butter and olive oil in a medium saucepan set over a medium heat until the butter foams. Add the prepared parsnips, potato, onion and garlic and season with salt and pepper. Toss the vegetables and seasoning in the fat until well coated, then cover with a piece of parchment or greaseproof paper. Pop the lid on the saucepan and cook on a **very gentle heat** to sweat the vegetables. If the heat is too high the vegetables may stick to the bottom of the saucepan and burn. Cook for 15–20 minutes, until some of the vegetables are beginning to soften at the edges and collapse.

2 Add the stock and bring to a simmer again but **don't boil**, as some of the stock may evaporate and the soup will be too thick. Cover with the lid and continue to cook on that gentle heat until the vegetables are completely tender. This will take about 15 minutes.

3 Purée the soup to a silky-smooth consistency. Taste and correct the seasoning. At this point I sometimes add a little more stock or a splash of cream to correct the consistency and the flavour.

4 Serve in hot bowls with a teaspoon of harissa and a drizzle of your best extra virgin olive oil on each serving.

Spiced Beef

30g black peppercorns

30g allspice berries

6g star anise

4 whole cloves

1 cinnamon stick

100g fine sea salt

100g dark brown muscovado or
demerara sugar

1.35kg silverside of beef

To serve

salad of shaved cauliflower and
Brussels sprouts (page 249)

I only discovered spiced beef when I came to live in Cork, and how dear it is to the city and county. In some parts of the country spiced beef only appears at Christmas, but in Cork it is available and eaten year round. The beef is equally good served hot or cold. In this meal I am serving it cold with the shaved cauliflower salad, which pairs beautifully with it. I like to serve the beef a few days after Christmas, when the turkey and ham may be losing some of their appeal. The cooked spiced beef will keep tightly covered in the fridge for 2 weeks. **Serves 8–10**

1 Grind the peppercorns, allspice, star anise, cloves and cinnamon stick in a spice grinder to a fine powder, then mix with the salt and sugar. Massage this spice mixture into the meat. Place the meat and any remaining spices in a container that it fits into snugly. Cover tightly and refrigerate overnight.

2 The next day, give the beef a turn in the container and cover and chill once again. The beef needs to marinate and spice for five to seven days for the flavours to penetrate the meat and I like to turn it every day. After a couple of days the spice mixture will become liquid as the salt and spices draw juices out of the meat.

3 To cook the beef, place it in a saucepan that it fits into snugly and pour in all the liquid and spice in the container. Top up the saucepan with enough cold water to cover the beef. Bring to a simmer, cover and simmer gently for about 2½ hours. **Keep an eye on the water level in the saucepan and top up if necessary, making sure the level of the water is always higher than the beef.** When cooked, a skewer should go through the beef with just a little resistance. Remove from the water, allow to cool and then chill.

4 Slice the cold beef very thinly and serve with the shaved cauliflower salad.

Salad of Shaved Cauliflower and Brussels Sprouts with Red Onions, Raisins and Parmesan

50g raisins

50g unskinned hazelnuts

1 small cauliflower

12 Brussels sprouts, peeled

225g red onion, peeled

8 tablespoons Caesar dressing
  (page 250)

2–4 tablespoons extra virgin olive oil

50g grated Parmesan

sea salt and freshly ground
  black pepper

2 tablespoons pomegranate seeds
  (optional)

I love serving this salad in winter and I particularly like it with spiced beef, but it is also excellent with ham or cured meats such as salamis or chorizos and with coarse pâtés and terrines. Scraps of leftover turkey or ham can be folded through the salad and makes leftovers into what I call 'bestovers'. It is certainly interesting enough to serve just as it is as a starter in another meal, in which case I would serve grilled sourdough bread drizzled with olive oil (page 16) to accompany it. **Serves 6–8**

1 Preheat the oven to 200°C.
2 Place the raisins in a heatproof bowl, pour over enough boiling water to cover them and soak for 1 hour.
3 Place the hazelnuts on a roasting tray and roast in the oven for about 15 minutes, until the nuts are roasted to a golden colour and the skins are starting to lift. Remove from the oven and allow to cool. Place the nuts in a clean towel and rub off as many of the skins as possible, then chop the nuts coarsely.
4 Trim the outside leaves and tough stalk off the cauliflower and discard or reserve for a vegetable stock. Break or cut the flower into florets. Cut the cauliflower florets into slices about 5mm thick and place in a large bowl. Slice the sprouts and red onion even more thinly and add to the cauliflower. Drain the soaking water off the raisins and discard. Add the raisins to the cauliflower. Add the Caesar dressing and half of the olive oil and toss thoroughly but gently. Add three-quarters of the grated Parmesan and mix again. Taste and correct the seasoning.
5 Spread the salad out in a large shallow bowl or plate and sprinkle on the hazelnuts and pomegranate seeds (if using). Add a final drizzle of oil and sprinkle the remaining Parmesan over the salad and it is ready to serve, though it will happily sit for an hour before serving.

Caesar Dressing

1 x 50g tin of anchovies

2 egg yolks, preferably free-range

1 garlic clove, peeled and crushed
   to a paste

2 tablespoons freshly squeezed
   lemon juice

1 tablespoon Worcestershire sauce

1 tablespoon Tabasco sauce

generous pinch of dry English
   mustard powder

small pinch of salt

175ml sunflower oil

50ml extra virgin olive oil

approx. 50ml cold water

What a useful and flavoursome dressing this is and it's perfect for the cauliflower salad on page 249. **Serves 6–8**

1 I make this dressing in a food processor, but it can also be made very quickly by hand. The food processor achieves a smoother and creamier result, though, which I prefer.

2 Drain the anchovies and crush them lightly with a fork. Put into the bowl of the food processor with the egg yolks, garlic, lemon juice, Worcestershire and Tabasco sauce, mustard powder and salt. Whizz all the ingredients together. With the motor running, add the oils in a slow trickle at first, then a little faster as the emulsion forms and the sauce begins to appear creamy. Finally, add in enough of the water to make a spreadable consistency like thick pouring cream. Taste and correct the seasoning: this dressing should be highly flavoured.

3 Store the dressing in a covered container in the fridge. I find that after two days the flavour becomes overly strong and loses its freshness.

Orange and Passion Fruit Granita with Mango, Banana and Lime

5 ripe passion fruit

450ml freshly squeezed orange juice

110g + 2 teaspoons caster sugar

1 ripe mango

1 lime

2 bananas

fresh mint leaves when in season

This is a light and refreshing end to a meal and I find that it is particularly well appreciated after Christmas, when the richer and much-loved traditional flavours are perhaps starting to wear a bit thin. You do not need an ice cream machine to make the granita, just a little commitment to giving it the odd stir as it freezes. The resulting coarse texture is charming and invigorating. **Serves 6–8**

1 Cut the passion fruit in half and pass the pulp and juice through a fine sieve to remove the seeds. The more of the pulp and juice you extract, the more flavoursome the granita will be. Mix this liquid with the orange juice and 110g of sugar and stir with a whisk to dissolve the sugar completely.

2 Place the mixture in a large flat-bottomed airtight container and freeze. When the mixture starts to **freeze around the edges**, use a fork or whisk to break it up into a pulp. Refreeze and continue this process **three more times**, by which time you will have a coarse granita-type texture.

3 Peel the mango and cut into neat slices or dice. Zest and juice the lime and add to the mango along with 2 teaspoons of sugar. Stir gently to encourage the sugar to dissolve. Taste to check that the level of sweetness is to your liking, adding a little more sugar if needed. Chill for 30 minutes or more. Peel and slice the bananas and add to the mango just before serving.

4 Serve the granita with the mango and banana and some of the juice and scatter over the mint if it is in season.

Larder

Olive Oil

Olive oil is a crucial ingredient in my cooking. I always use extra virgin olive oil regardless of whether I am serving it cold or heating it to use it as a cooking fat. The only other ingredient that I know of that has such an immediate and dramatically positive effect on the flavour of your food is using real butter as distinct from a butter substitute.

Some olive oil is of poor quality and will have a disastrous effect on the flavour of the foods served with it. A good bottle of extra virgin olive oil costs considerably less than a bottle of average wine and will have a dramatic effect on the taste of your food. Search out an oil that you enjoy – this is a classic case of the need to shop carefully. An independent shopkeeper is more likely to be able to dispense the information you need to know about the oil. Where is the oil from? Is it cold pressed? When were the olives harvested? For most people the label on the bottle tells you very little, in much the same way that labels on bottles of wine are a mystery to all except the experts. So you need to consult the experts and hopefully your shopkeeper will be able to guide you and translate the rather vague details on the bottle label into a language that you and I can understand.

Parchment Paper

I often use a sheet of parchment paper to cover and protect food while it is cooking or when it is finished cooking. I also use it as a non-stick aid in certain cases, particularly when cooking meringues, cooling praline and shaping chocolate. When used in these instances, the paper can often be dusted off and reused.

Occasionally I dampen the paper under the tap and then gently wring out most of the water sticking to the paper. The paper becomes pliable and can then be moulded over a dish of food to protect the contents. At that point the paper will be covered with a fine mist of water bubbles that will create a steamy atmosphere over foods that I don't want to develop a crust, such as mashed potatoes or a bowl of stew being kept warm before going to the table.

Puff Pastry

I have never found a puff pastry to buy that is as good as one you make yourself. The first time you make it the process may seem daunting, but once you have absorbed the formula, then it really is not such a trial. The flaky and sweetly buttery nature of the pastry is a special thing and worth every moment of anxiety you might have with your first attempt. The pastry takes about 90 minutes from start to finish, but the time you spend handling it is no longer than 15 minutes. The rest of the time it is just chilling in the fridge. You end up with a pastry with 729 layers, and each of those layers contributes to the lightness and crispness of the result and hopefully to your pleasure on eating it.

If you are going to freeze some of the pastry, do it sooner rather than later so as to preserve the fresh flavour of the butter. **Makes 1kg**

450g baker's or strong white flour
pinch of salt
250ml ice-cold water
450g butter, cold from the fridge

1 Sieve the flour and salt into a large bowl. Add almost all of the water, and with your hand, mix to form a dough, adding the remaining water if it refuses to come together.

2 The dough will not look particularly attractive or smooth at this stage. A soft dough, or détrempe, as it is called, will make a flabby pastry that will not rise with straight sides when cooked later. If your détrempe is too dry, the pastry is more likely to crack when you are rolling and folding it.

3 Cover the détrempe by wrapping it in greaseproof or parchment paper or cling film, or slip it into a large plastic bag. Chill for 30 minutes.

4 When the détrempe is chilled, dust the worktop with flour and roll the dough into a 30cm square.

5 Place the cold butter, wrapper removed, in a strong plastic bag and bash it with your rolling pin to achieve a rectangular slab that is pliable but still chilled. The slab should be about 13cm wide and 17cm long. You will probably have to shape the butter a bit with your hands, but don't allow the butter to warm up or start to melt.

6 Place the butter on the middle of the square of dough and fold in the edges of the dough as if making a neat parcel. The butter should be completely enveloped – no butter should be visible.

7 Now roll the dough and butter 'parcel' into a rectangle about 22cm wide and 45cm long. What is really important, though, is that the sides and ends of the pastry are straight so that when you fold the pastry, all of the edges meet in flush lines. If your pastry looks misshapen, apply pressure with your rolling pin wherever necessary to achieve a regular shape.

8 Brush the excess flour off the surface of the pastry with a pastry brush, then neatly and precisely fold the dough into three, as if folding a business letter. This is crucial, and

lining up the edges of the dough neatly is also crucial. With folds and edges carefully aligned, the pastry will rise up straight later. If not carefully aligned, the rising pastry has a tendency to tumble off to one side or other. You now have three layers in your pastry.

9 Give the dough a 90 degree clockwise turn. It should now look like a book ready to be opened on your worktop. Roll out again into a rectangle as before, fold in three again and seal at the edges by pressing gently with your rolling pin. Your pastry now has nine layers. Brush off the excess flour. Place in a plastic bag and chill for at least 30 minutes.

10 Now the pastry has had two single rolls or one double roll. It needs two more of these double rolls, allowing a 30-minute rest and chill between each double roll.

11 Chill the pastry after the final roll for at least 30 minutes.

12 The pastry is now ready to be rolled again for cutting, shaping and cooking.

Chicken Stock

There are a few important rules to remember when making any stock. Choose a saucepan that the ingredients fit snugly into. If your saucepan is too big, you will have too much water and will end up with a watery stock that is lacking in flavour. Always pour cold water over the ingredients, as the cold water will draw the flavour out of the bones and vegetables as it comes up to the boil. Remember, it is the liquid you are after here, so getting the flavour into the liquid is vital. Bring the contents of the pan slowly to the boil and then only allow the stock to simmer gently as it cooks. If it boils, it will loosen solid particles from the meat and vegetables and your stock will taste rather muddy and look cloudy. I prefer not to cover the stock when it is cooking, as it can cause the stock to cloud up. A rich and well-flavoured chicken stock can be achieved in two hours. I find that cooking the stock for hours on end makes it too strong. The stock will keep in the fridge for a few days or can be frozen. Makes 3 litres

2–3 raw or cooked chicken
   carcasses or a mixture of both
giblets from the chicken, i.e. neck,
   heart, gizzard (optional)
1 onion, sliced
1 leek, split in two
1 outside stick of celery
1 carrot, sliced
a few fresh parsley stalks
1 sprig of fresh thyme
6 peppercorns
approx. 3.4 litres cold water

Chop or break up the chicken carcasses. Put all the ingredients in a saucepan and cover with the **cold water**. Bring slowly up to the boil and skim the fat off the top with a tablespoon. **Simmer very gently** for 2–3 hours, uncovered. Strain and remove any remaining fat. If you need a stronger flavour, boil down the liquid in an open pan to reduce by one-third or one-half the volume. Do not add salt.

Curry Powder

This is the blend of spices that I use to make a curry powder. I find it to be very well balanced and I store it in a tightly sealed container. **Makes 35g**

2 tablespoons whole
    coriander seeds
1 tablespoon whole cumin seeds
1 dessertspoon chilli flakes (add
    more if you want a hotter mix)
2 teaspoons whole
    black peppercorns
1 teaspoon brown mustard seeds
4 whole cloves
1 teaspoon whole fenugreek seeds
1 teaspoon ground turmeric

1   Place a heavy frying pan over a medium heat. When it is hot, add all of the spices except the fenugreek and turmeric. Cook, stirring, until the spices start to release their aroma, change colour lightly and smell lightly roasted. Add the fenugreek and turmeric and cook for a further 10 seconds.

2   Remove from the pan immediately and allow to cool before grinding to a fine powder in a clean coffee grinder or spice grinder. Store the spices in a clean sealed container such as a jam jar. Keep them in a cool dark place and ideally use within a couple of weeks.

Mayonnaise

Where would we be without mayonnaise? What would we serve with cold salmon and lobster? How would we create a tartar sauce or an aioli?

A lot of fuss is made of the difficulty and length of time involved in making your own mayonnaise, to the point that many cooks are scared off by the process. If you take your time and slowly whisk the oil onto the eggs, you will not have a problem. If I am making a single batch of the recipe I will make it by hand, but if multiplying the quantity I use a food processor. The machine-made sauce tends to be thicker and can be softened to the required consistency with a little water.

Remember that poor oil and battery eggs will make a poor mayonnaise. The better quality the eggs are, the more difficult it is to curdle the mayonnaise. **Serves 6–10**

2 egg yolks
1 dessertspoon white wine vinegar
¼ teaspoon Dijon mustard
sea salt and freshly ground black
    pepper
250ml oil (sunflower, peanut or olive
    or a mixture – I use about half
    olive and half peanut)

1   Place the egg yolks, vinegar, mustard and a pinch of salt and pepper in a bowl. **Drop the oil very slowly** onto the egg mix, whisking all the time. The mixture will gradually start to thicken. You can start to add the oil a little bit more quickly now, but don't get carried away by your success, as caution is needed right up until all the oil has been whisked in. Taste and correct the seasoning.

2   If the mayonnaise curdles, it will become quite thin and oily on top. If this happens, put another egg yolk into a clean bowl and whisk in the curdled mayonnaise one teaspoon at a time until it emulsifies again.

3   Store in a clean jar in the fridge for up to a week.

Tomato Purée

This is a marvellous recipe for preserving the flavour of ripe summer tomatoes for the long months when the tomatoes are pale, bullet like and have a miserably thin flavour. Buy the ripest vine tomatoes you can get for this purée. I make lots of this around the end of August and into September and freeze it to keep me going through the winter. If you don't have time to make it when the tomatoes are at their best, and ironically their cheapest, you can just freeze the tomatoes, defrost them at a later stage and proceed with the recipe. In fact, freezing ripe tomatoes is another great way to have good tomato flavour at your disposal throughout the year. When defrosted they peel really easily and will have retained that fabulous late summer taste. Search for organic tomatoes at farmers markets or at your vegetable shop. It is not unusual to get excellent value for money when the glut of tomatoes happens at the end of the summer. So think deep, deep red colour and you will be rewarded all year long with a little of the summer trapped in your freezer. I use the purée in stews, soups and sauces. The basic purée can be reduced to thicken to make tomato paste.
Makes about 1 litre

900g very ripe tomatoes
1 small onion, peeled and chopped
1 teaspoon caster sugar
a good pinch of salt and a few
   twists of black pepper

Cut the tomatoes into quarters and put into a stainless steel saucepan with the onion, sugar, salt and freshly ground black pepper. Cook, covered, on a gentle heat for about 30 minutes, until the tomatoes are soft (no water needed). Pass through the fine blade of a mouli-legume or a nylon sieve. Allow to get cold, then refrigerate or freeze.

How to Peel a Tomato

It is crucial that tomatoes are really ripe before peeling them, both for flavour and ease of peeling.

   Remove the stalks from the tomatoes. With a small knife, make a shallow cross-shaped cut where the stalk was. This cut encourages the skins to lift off. Bring enough water to cover the tomatoes to the boil. Pour the **still-boiling water** over to submerge the tomatoes completely. **Count to 10 seconds** and immediately pour off all the boiling water. Refresh the tomatoes in cold water for a few seconds. Pour off the cold water, then simply peel off the skins.

Preserved Lemons

Salty and sour preserved lemons have always been associated with the food of North Africa, but cooks have now realised that the tart flavour of the preserved citrus fruit has a place in many cuisines. There are several ways to make the preserve and I am giving you a recipe for a quick but nonetheless delicious result. ***Makes 1 jar***

4 lemons
4 tablespoons coarse sea salt
approx. 150ml sunflower oil

1. Use a small sharp knife to make a cut in the lemon skin from top to bottom. Make eight cuts in each lemon. The skin should be pierced but preferably not the soft juicy lemon flesh. Rub some of the salt into the incisions and place the fruit in a saucepan with the remaining salt. Cover with cold water and bring to a simmer. You may need to place a small plate or saucer on top of the lemons to keep them submerged in the salty water. Simmer very gently for about 1 hour, until the flesh is really tender but not soft and mushy. Remove from the water and allow to cool completely.

2. Cut the lemons in half from top to bottom, scoop out all of the soft flesh and discard it. Place the strips of skin in a clean jar and cover with the sunflower oil. Make sure the lemon is completely submerged in the oil. The lemons can now be stored in the fridge for months.

Fresh Lemonade

In this book I use a lot of lemon zest as a final seasoning on some of the dishes, so I wanted to include a recipe to make sure you are not left with lemons full of juice and no use for them. This fresh lemonade is quick, easy and delicious. The herb can be either mint or lemon balm – both are equally good here. Lemon basil, a herb I adore, is also great here but more difficult to find.

This lemonade could become the base for an adult cocktail with the addition of a sensible splash of gin or vodka. ***Serves 6***

juice of 4 lemons
100g caster sugar
25g fresh mint, lemon balm or lemon basil leaves
1 litre still or sparkling water

Place the lemon juice, sugar and herb leaves in a blender. Whizz to chop the leaves finely and dissolve the sugar. Decant into a large jug, add the water and stir well. Serve over lots of ice.

How to Cook French, Flat or Scarlet Runner Beans

The crucial rule that applies to cooking all green vegetables applies here: once the vegetables go into the salted boiling water, do not replace the saucepan lid. **Serves 4–6 as a vegetable accompaniment**

1.2 litres water

2–3 teaspoons salt

900g beans, topped and tailed and
   cut into 5cm pieces on the bias

25g butter or 2 tablespoons olive oil

sea salt and freshly ground
   black pepper

1 Bring the water to a rolling boil, then add the salt and the prepared beans. Cook, **uncovered**, for about 6 minutes, then taste one of the beans. The texture should be firm but not in any way tough or 'squeaky'. 'Yielding' is perhaps the best word to describe the texture. Strain the beans immediately through a sieve or colander.

2 Place the beans back in the empty but still hot saucepan and add the butter or olive oil and a few grinds of black pepper. Stir to glaze the beans and taste one to see if a little more salt is required. Serve immediately in a hot serving dish.

How to Cook Lobster

This method of cooking lobster is recommended by the RSPCA.

I find the flesh to be tender and succulent as a result of this form of cooking. The alternative methods for cooking the fish – plunging the fish into boiling water or using a knife on the live fish – tend to make the flesh tougher.

Choose heavy and active live fish with a nice inky navy colour, a hard shell and both claws intact.

The fish should be a minimum of 700g (1½lb) in weight. Avoid fish that are too big, as I find them to have less flavour and tougher flesh.

The method described can be used for cooking just one lobster or a larger quantity.

Allow per lobster:

sea salt

4 slices of peeled carrot

4 slices of peeled onion

1 celery stick

bouquet garni (1 bay leaf, parsley and thyme stalks)

250ml white wine

250ml water, plus tepid water to cover the fish

1 Place the live fish in a saucepan and cover with tepid water. Add 170g of salt per every 2 litres of water. Cover the pot, place on a medium heat and bring to just under the boiling point. The lobsters die at about 44°C (112°F). The lobsters will have changed colour to a speckled coral colour.

2 Discard all the water. Add the vegetables, bouquet garni, wine and 250ml of extra water and place a tight-fitting lid on the pot. Bring to a gentle boil and steam the fish for about another 15 minutes. Have a look at the fish to check that they have completely changed colour and are a bright coral colour all over. Give them a few more minutes if necessary.

3 Remove from the pot and reserve the cooking liquid for soups, sauces, etc.

4 The lobster is now ready for various preparations.

Harissa

I keep a jar of this hot and spicy North African-inspired paste in the fridge most of the time. It is a really useful condiment for seasoning and marinating and for adding a little heat to certain dishes.

I use it with grilled lamb, pork and chicken, with oily fish such as salmon and mackerel, on hard-boiled eggs and in an omelette, and stirred through a mayonnaise as a sauce or through olive oil to make a slightly hot vinaigrette for crisp, cool salad leaves.

I use medium-hot chillies such as cayenne, jalapeño or serrano to give a level of heat that is obvious but not scorching. **Makes 1 small jar**

6 medium-hot fresh red chillies,
    such as cayenne, jalapeño or
    serrano
8 garlic cloves, peeled and crushed
    to a paste
1½ tablespoons tomato purée
3 teaspoons cumin seeds, roasted
    and ground
3 teaspoons coriander seeds,
    roasted and ground
6 tablespoons extra virgin olive oil
1 teaspoon red wine vinegar or
    lemon juice
3 tablespoons chopped fresh
    coriander leaves
sea salt and freshly ground
    black pepper
pinch of caster sugar

1 Preheat the oven to 200°C.
2 Place the chillies on a small roasting tray and roast in the oven for about 20 minutes. The skins will be blackening and blistering and coming away from the flesh. Place the roasted chillies in a bowl, seal tightly with cling film and allow to cool. When cool, peel off the skins and slit the chillies to remove the seeds. You just want the roasted flesh of the chilli for the harissa.
3 Place the chillies in a food processor or use a pestle and mortar. Add the garlic, tomato purée and ground spices and process to a smooth-ish purée. Gradually add the oil and vinegar. Add the chopped coriander leaves and season to taste, adding a tiny pinch of sugar if you feel the flavour needs a lift. The taste should be strong, hot and pungent.
4 Stored in a covered container such as a jam jar in the fridge, the harissa will keep perfectly for several months.

Index